THREE AMERICAN EMPIRES

INTERPRETATIONS OF AMERICAN HISTORY

★ ★ ★ JOHN HIGHAM AND BRADFORD PERKINS, EDITORS

THREE AMERICAN EMPIRES

EDITED BY

John J. TePaske
The Ohio State University

HARPER & ROW, PUBLISHERS
NEW YORK, EVANSTON, AND LONDON

THREE AMERICAN EMPIRES

Library of Congress Catalog Card Number: 67-17641

CONTENTS

v

Indian Policy in Colonial America

Colonial Culture and Learning:
Spanish and English America in the Eighteenth Century

EDITORS' INTRODUCTION

This volume—and companions in the series, "Interpretations of American History"—makes a special effort to cope with one of the basic dilemmas confronting every student of history. On the one hand, historical knowledge shares a characteristic common to all appraisals of human affairs. It is partial and selective. It picks out some features and facts of a situation while ignoring others that may be equally pertinent. The more selective an interpretation is, the more memorable and widely applicable it can be. On the other hand, history has to provide what nothing else does: a total estimate, a multifaceted synthesis, of man's experience in particular times and places. To study history, therefore, is to strive simultaneously for a clear, selective focus and for an integrated, over-all view.

In that spirit, each book of the series aims to resolve the varied literature on a major topic or event into a meaningful whole. One interpretation, we believe, does not deserve as much of a student's attention as another simply because they are in conflict. Instead of contriving a balance between opposing views, or choosing polemical material simply to create an appearance of controversy, Professor TePaske has exercised his own judgment on the relative importance of different aspects or interpretations of a problem. We have asked him to select some of what he considers the best, most persuasive writings bearing on the three American empires, indicating in the introductory essay and headnotes his reasons for considering these accounts convincing or significant. When appropriate, he has also brought out the relation between older and more recent approaches to the subject. The editor's own competence and experience in the field enable him to provide a sense of order and to indicate the evolution and complexity of interpretations. He is, then, like other editors in this series, an informed participant rather than a mere observer, a student sharing with other students the results of his own investigations of the literature on a crucial phase of American development.

JOHN HIGHAM
BRADFORD PERKINS

vii

INTRODUCTION

I

The colonization of America was undeniably a European venture, but whether the American empires were simply an extension of Europe or whether the New World environment transformed European ideas and institutions into distinctly American phenomena is open to question. Spain, Portugal, England, France, and the Netherlands all played a vital role in opening and settling the New World, and perhaps this is the crucial factor: Although the direction of colonial life was unquestionably European, it was more particularly Spanish, Portuguese, French, English, and Dutch.

As the first nation to found permanent colonies in America, Spain created the vastest empire—from Tierra del Fuego at the southern tip of South America to frontier outposts on the east and west coasts of the present-day United States. In 1500 Portugal established a tenuous foothold along the coast of Brazil and after 1530 committed itself to a more ambitious colonial endeavor in that vast land. French fishermen and fur traders plied the North Atlantic coast and the Saint Lawrence Valley in the sixteenth century; after Samuel de Champlain founded Quebec in 1608, they expanded into other parts of Canada, the Great Lakes area, the Mississippi Basin, and the Antilles. Initially dwarfed in its imperial efforts by other European powers, England gained a foothold in the West Indies and settled the thirteen colonies on the North American mainland. After failures in New Amsterdam and Brazil, the Dutch clung to a few islands in the Antilles and a bit of Guiana in South America.

Despite the contributions of the Portuguese and the Dutch to the New World, this volume is restricted to the English in the thirteen colonies, the French in Canada, and the Spanish in New Spain and Peru. The choice is limited for good reasons. These three nations not only dominated European affairs in the sixteenth, seventeenth, and eighteenth centuries, but all together they encompassed the largest territorial expanse in America. Moreover, each had the requisites to support an overseas empire—a burgeoning population, restless spirit, wealth, and an effective central government.

II

The similarities and differences in the three American empires have caused considerable debate, stimulated largely by Herbert E. Bolton's presidential address before the American Historical Association in 1932. Bolton argued for an "Epic of Greater America"; for American history which transcended narrow national or lingual lines and embraced the entire Western Hemisphere. Pleading for more emphasis on unities, he observed: "Likenesses in the colonial systems were more striking than differences." Each colonial power imposed feudal or neo-feudal institutions—the Spanish *encomienda,* the French seigneury, and the English proprietary grant; each subjected their New World settlements to a mercantilistic policy; each adopted slavery; each founded universities. Also, colonials in all three empires had to adjust to the unknown American environment, making their way in a strange land as best they could.

Bolton's thesis met a good deal of opposition. In the vanguard of the dissenters was Edmundo O'Gorman, the Mexican philosopher-historian. He replied that there were similarities in American colonial history simply because all men were born and reared, ate and worked. In short, these were the "unities of Nature and not of human nature, which is the essence of history." Bolton's emphasis on likenesses was meaningless, for it "relegated to oblivion that spiritual complex which gives body to a historical entity." The reality of American colonial history lay not in the similarity, but in the uniqueness of the various cultures and institutions. "Spanish colonization," O'Gorman argued, "is animated by a medieval spirit; whatever it contains that is modern is a blemish in it. Anglo-American colonization is of pure modern inspiration; whatever it contains that is medieval is, in it and for it, an unjustified limitation." In the end he saw no sense in speaking of a "common history" of America.

To overstress the rigidity of Bolton's and O'Gorman's views would be an injustice to both and leave us with a much too strongly dialectical approach to comparative colonial history. That is not the intent of this volume. If men are a mixture of saint and devil, if they act from a wide variety of motives, if many factors influence their responses, so too American colonial history is exceedingly complex and a mixture of both unities and diversities. In some cases, as Bolton argued, England, France, and Spain responded to colonial problems in the same way; in other cases they pursued widely different courses. To take one position over the other would merely inhibit better understanding of American colonial development, and for comparative history there are already many obstacles to effective analysis.

One of the biggest impediments to meaningful comparison is the lack of a proper time sense or historical empathy by which we put ourselves in the place of the principal actors. That Spain carved out her empire in the sixteenth century and England and France in the seventeenth is fundamental if we are to determine the direction of colonial life in America. Spanish colonization must be understood as a medieval phenomenon; England and France, with a century intervening before the development of their empires, had time to take on a more modern outlook. In a sense, Spain became the victim of an historical accident: The fall of Granada early in 1492 coinciding with the discovery of America a few months later was decisive in the formation of a Spanish colonial mystique, for it enabled the Spaniard to transfer to America the spirit of the seven-hundred-year Reconquest—the quest for glory, souls, and the material rewards of military victory in land, treasure, and title. This same historical accident also made it virtually impossible for Spain to develop the more modern bourgeois values of thrift, hard work, and austerity, incipient in some areas of the Iberian peninsula.

But timing is not the only factor to consider. France and Spain brought Roman Catholicism with them to the New World rather than Protestantism. That England developed a parliamentary tradition at the same time as her rivals epitomized absolute monarchy is essential for perceptive analysis. The personalities of policy-makers, ministers, and colonial administrators; the legal systems of each colonial power; and the quality and quantity of the emigrant from the mother country are also important influences.

A second obstacle to comparative colonial history is failure to understand the differences in the climate and geography of America. Except for their Antillian possessions, France and England developed their colonial empires in a temperate climate. Geographic barriers did not impede movement. French missionaries and fur traders traveled easily along the Great Lakes and western rivers to reach their Indian villages and trading posts. English settlers could move freely from one colony to another along the Atlantic coast, while the Appalachian mountains, the most significant barrier to English expansion westward, never proved a major obstacle. For Spanish America, geography was not as kind. Deserts, mountains, and dense jungle isolated one section of the empire from another, made administration difficult, and inhibited movement. In fact, the utter vastness of Spanish America distinguished it from its French and English counterparts.

A third barrier to sensitive comparative study is the inability to assess fundamental differences in the Indian problem. All three colonial powers had to deal with indigenous populations, but conditions in English and French America differed greatly from those in Spanish America. French and English settlers encountered relatively small populations of Indians with very primitive cultures, but the Spanish conquistadores and their progeny faced the highly developed Aztecs (Mexicas), Mayas, Chibchas, and Incas with their immensely complex social, economic, political, and religious institutions. Although epidemics and mistreatment decimated the native population, Spain incorporated the indigenes into the colonial order, converted them, and attempted to Hispanicize them. At the same time they exploited the Indians in mines, haciendas, and workshops (obrajes). Unlike the English who pushed the Indian westward or the French who left him alone, virtually unsullied by all European institutions except liquor and the Christian religion, the Spanish ordered their society in such a way as to make the Indian a part of it. Whether the English and French would have responded in a similar way in similar circumstances is a fundamental question for comparative study.

A fourth problem in dealing effectively with the three American empires is determining what can be usefully compared. Broad generalizations based on the three imperial structures taken as a whole can have few rewards, for within their own empires the three European powers developed many different types of settlements which, in themselves, present strong contrasts. New England differed in many ways from Virginia or Georgia; in Spanish America the frontier cities of Buenos Aires and Santiago de Chile must be distinguished from the flourishing centers of Lima and Mexico City. Useful comparisons can be made only when similar areas or institutions are placed side by side at similar stages in development. Spanish Saint Augustine, English Savannah, and French

Mobile are comparable, but must not be put in the same categories with Bogotá, Boston, and Quebec. We might compare the French intendant with the Spanish viceroy, but not with the English sheriff. To go one step further, one might argue, with some justification, that valid comparisons can only be made where the colonial powers encountered similar problems, responded to the same conditions, and acted in the same point in time. This inevitably leads one to the Caribbean area in the seventeenth century, but this volume ranges more widely and reflects the similarities and differences in colonial institutions and ideas within wider geographical and chronological limits.

The last obstacle to objective comparative study is moral indignation, a factor which could interfere with the rational, empathic observation of any historical phenomenon. For example, the predisposition to view slavery or communism as absolute moral evils may well blind us to their place and meaning in history. So it is with the history of the European powers in the New World. Moral preconceptions about England, France, and Spain may cloud our judgment and jade our thinking. In many cases the atmosphere of moral self-righteousness has already colored our views with Spain being the principal victim and England the chief beneficiary. Familiarly cast as barbaric, bigoted, greedy, lustful, and obscurantist, the Spaniard in the New World has been morally castigated since the middle of the sixteenth century. Orthodox and absolutist, the embodiment of her medieval virtues and defects, Spain became an easy target for those who preferred to use a more modern standard of judgment based on a belief in progress, toleration, individual freedom, and popular sovereignty. Within this latter framework, England, in America, assumed a special moral aura taking on the very qualities Spain denied or lacked. French America came to lie somewhere between the two poles. But even if we make our judgments within this more modern framework, we can use the broader perspectives of comparative study to put these traditional views to a test. This is not to argue that the historian has no role as a moral critic; in the end this may well be the most valuable result of comparative history. It is simply a warning that such criticism should only be made after careful comparative study.

III

The selections in this volume are an introduction to the vast realm of comparative colonial history. Representing the work of specialists in anthropology, history, literature, and sociology, the essays demonstrate various approaches to the American colonial past. The first three sections

—on concepts of empire, colonial society, and Indian policy—emphasize the differences in the various colonial endeavors in America and attempt to answer in part why these differences occurred. The last section—on colonial intellectual life in the eighteenth century—stresses Bolton's unity of American history.

The three selections on the concept of empire use the ideas and institutions of the Old World as a backdrop for colonization of the New. In his essay, Eric Wolf sees the Spanish quest for an overseas utopia as a dominant motive, both for the early friars with their desire to create an unsullied, Christian Valhalla among the natives, and for the early conquistadores with their search for titles, land, and riches. For Wolf, the Spanish conquest of America also represented an extension of Spain's medieval heritage—of the seven-hundred-year fight against the infidel Moors.

From sixteenth-century writings, Howard Mumford Jones builds an ingenious argument for the growth of English ideas toward colonization. An eclectic, he sees many factors interacting to create the English colonizing ethos. One of these—and perhaps a bit overemphasized—is the Irish experience. Many Englishmen, Jones argues, fought in Ireland during the sixteenth century and came to know it as a harsh land inhabited by barbarians, or at least so the chroniclers and soldiers who returned from the Irish wars pictured it. Thus, the Irish experience was negative conditioning which led the early settlers in America to expect the worst. On the more positive side, dispelling the effect of the Irish wars, was the promotion literature appealing to the quest for glory, the need to convert the heathen, the rewards to be reaped from trade, the problem of surplus population, and the opporutnities for English patriots and expansionists. England's imperial idea, Jones believes, was a mixture of inconsistent and contradictory motives. "America," he observes (in dispute of some traditional views), "did not descend directly from Eden."

In the third essay in this section Kenneth D. McRae stresses the political ideas and institutions of Louis XIV's France as the crucial factor in the development of French Canada. All previous attempts to mold a colonial idea, if indeed there were any, failed. New France, he argues, "bore the imprint" of the Sun King and his finance minister, Jean Baptiste Colbert, whose policies defined the French concept of empire. Aiming to make New France a deliberate projection of the mother country, a neofeudal creation, they pursued a program best calculated to achieve their goal—the seigneurial system, a colonial government regulated precisely by ministers in Paris, and a highly selective, restrictive immigration policy.

Implicit in the three selections is the basic issue of heritage versus environment as an influence on colonial ventures. Obviously both factors played a significant role in defining the imperial ideal of Spain, England, and France, but we must go further. How significant were propaganda and promotion literature in developing a concept of empire for the three nations? Was it as vital a factor as their past history and their political, social, economic, and religious institutions? How important was the American environment and Indian problem in transforming the patterns of life and ideals the colonists carried with them to the New World? With Spanish colonization essentially the product of the later medieval period and French and English settlement of a more modern age, to what extent did timing change the concept of empire for each power? Was timing as significant as Wolf believes? In the end, how important was the European milieu in the creation of an imperial idea?

The second section on colonial society is less closely knit but high-lights the problems and rewards of comparative study. In his analysis of Mexican society in the seventeenth century, Irving A. Leonard stresses the infinite variety of classes and castes (as diverse and diffuse as the Baroque epoch of which they were a part). This kaleidoscopic mixture, however, did not prevent the society from being rigidly stratified and immobile with a minuscule, but all-powerful, white elite at the top. Leonard's description stands in sharp contrast to that of Jackson T. Main, who shows that English colonial society in the eighteenth century was classless, mobile, and white with no place in it for Indians or castes. Each author demonstrates that slaves were common to both social struc-tures and ranked at the bottom of the social ladder. But some scholars such as Frank Tannenbaum and Stanley Elkins have pointed out that the attitude toward and treatment of slaves varied greatly from empire to empire, creating still another problem for comparative analysis. In ap-proach, the two selections present an interesting contrast. Leonard's essay is that of the historian as sensitive humanist with long experience in literary and historical source materials; Main's discussion is that of the historian as social scientist whose work is statistically oriented and rooted in careful research in quantifiable data.

In his views on French colonial society, the sociologist Sigmund Dia-mond shows the breadth of the social scientist with his quest for patterns and generalizations. Diamond's emphasis is upon the seigneurial system as the critical factor in France's neofeudal experiment in Canada. Used first to encourage agriculture, the seigneury later served as a means of social and political control for the absolutist French government. If the king had had his way, he shows, French Canadian society would have been as rigidly stratified as that of France itself, or of Spanish America. But the attempt to mold a society of colonial subjects who would act in a manner prescribed in Paris, failed—why? Diamond argues that the open frontier and the scarcity of voluntary labor prevented full development of the seigneury and blocked royal attempts to dominate New France. His essay also poses a number of questions fundamental to the student of comparative colonial history. Could men make a new start in America without being burdened by past history? Was it possible for a king and his ministers 3000–5000 miles away to force their colonial subjects to act according to their desire? Could colonial society be organized in order to avoid the defects in the social system of the Old World, or did the king or his colonial subjects ever want this in the first place?

Analysis of Indian policy provides still another significant point of comparison for the New World settlements. Facing dense populations of Indians with complex institutions, Spain had the most difficult problem, and in his selection, J. H. Parry demonstrates how it was resolved. He gives particular attention to Spanish attempts to bring the Indian into its New World society—the feudal guardianships (*encomiendas*), the forced labor system, and the legal arrangements set up to protect and civilize the natives. Parry believes that the gulf between the Christian utopia envisaged by lawmakers in Spain and the realities of colonial life was far too wide to be bridged and, despite laws to prevent exploitation and abuse, Spain carved out its New World empire from the labor of the Indians. To a large degree they were Hispanicized and Christianized and given a place in Spanish society, but a place similar to that of the medieval serf.

In his discussion of French and English Indian policy in America, Francis Parkman did not, as Parry did, have the advantages of the findings of modern scholarship; yet for a nineteenth-century observer, he had shrewd insights. An apologist for the French in America, Parkman believed they were far more effective than the English in dealing with the Indians. After surviving the crisis of the Iroquois War, French Canadian bushrangers (*coureurs de bois*) and Jesuits moved into the western wilderness to trade for furs and to extend French influence on the frontier. They succeeded with the Indians, Parkman points out, because the absolutist central government laid down a single Indian policy for all Canada, because French Canadians were resilient and accommodating toward the Indians and because the lucrative fur trade depended upon good relations with the natives. The English failed, he believes, because of their difficulty in fashioning a consistent Indian policy for all thirteen colonies, the penchant of most English settlers to cling to their coastal settlements rather than cross the Appalachian barrier, and the emphasis upon agriculture and industry rather than upon the fur trade. Although Parkman may over-idealize French successes, his essay clearly delineates many of the variables in the formation of Indian policy in all the colonial empires—political organization, economic system, religion, geography, and values. Each, he demonstrates, must be weighed carefully.

A comparison of colonial culture during the eighteenth century provides a fitting conclusion to this volume and a convenient backdrop for the wars of independence in English and Spanish America. In his essay on the Enlightenment in the Spanish Empire, John Tate Lanning has discussed the development of new ideas and modern science in the University of San Carlos de Guatemala. Analyzing the theses of its students and the achievements of its faculty, he concludes that San Carlos was alive with the ideas of the Scientific Revolution and the Enlightenment and that most of its students and teachers had discarded Aristotelianism and scholasticism in favor of Cartesianism, Newtonianism, experimentation, and a belief in reason. Lanning emphasizes, too, that there was less cultural lag than is generally supposed between the acceptance of new ideas in the Old World and their transfer to the New; that the clergy was much more enlightened than is ordinarily assumed; and that Guatemalan savants, such as Narciso Esparragosa y Gallardo, were not only eclectic adapters of European ideas, but also made significant contributions in their own right.

In his selection on scientific thought in English America in the eighteenth century, Louis B. Wright ranges more widely over the colonial scene, but comes to the same general conclusions as Professor Lanning concerning the effect of the Scientific Revolution and the Enlightenment. Throughout the thirteen colonies, Wright points out, receptive scholars such as John and William Bartram, Jared Eliot, David Rittenhouse, and John Winthrop IV spread the latest advancements in European science. More than any other single figure, however, Benjamin Franklin represented the quintessence of the Enlightenment in English America. His questioning mind, taste for experimentation, belief in reason, and desire for a continuous dialogue on scientific matters bore testimony to his remarkable intellectual sophistication and to the penetration of the Enlightenment into the thirteen colonies. Lanning, we have seen, stresses the importance of the university as a breeding ground for the promotion of science and learning, while Wright feels activities outside the institutional setting were more important; but this is only a minor point of divergence as both authors demonstrate the similarities in cultural trends.

A discussion of French colonial culture in the eighteenth century has not been included here primarily because Canada became English in 1763 before the Enlightenment could take firm root and because, unlike the thirteen colonies and the Spanish Empire, Canada was not wracked by a war for independence. It should be stressed, however, that New France had its schools and scholars. Like Spanish America the clergy dominated intellectual and cultural life and again, like Spanish America, the atmosphere was not stifling, repressive, or obscurantist. In the eighteenth century educated French Canadians read widely from the playwrights

Corneille, Racine, and Molière; from the political theorists and philosophers Bossuet, Fénelon, and Pascal; and even a smattering from the *philosophes*. But, still, the new ideas of the Scientific Revolution and Enlightenment hardly touched Canada for, as Professor McRae has argued, New France lacked the "explosive potentiality" and the proper milieu for these ideas to take root.

IV

This brief introduction and the selections which follow explore only a few of the possible areas in comparative colonial history. Many other subjects deserve attention as well. The concept, structure, and functioning of colonial administration merits close analysis. Slavery took hold in the three American empires; comparative study of all aspects of this institution would reveal a great deal, not only about colonial society and economic life, but also about religious ideas and value systems. The church and religious beliefs, family makeup, demographic patterns, immigration, and economic systems are still other areas worthy of careful analysis.

Finally, what are the rewards of comparative study? If we follow the dictum of a Bolton to look for similarities or of an O'Gorman to look for differences, what will we hope to gain? Comparative study leads to more perceptive questioning and to more meaningful answers. Of any event, institution, or idea the historian inevitably asks the questions who, when, where, what, and how; but most significantly he asks why. If there were unities in the English, French, and Spanish colonial systems, *why* were they present? Was it a similar value system rooted in Western European tradition? Was it a common response to the New World environment? Was it a common drive for profits and power rooted in a mercantilistic philosophy? What role did envy and emulation play in the formation of unities? Or, if there were differences, why did these emerge? Were the cultural traditions and history of each nation so unique that they dictated a unique response to the New World environment? Did religious beliefs play a vital role? How crucial was timing in causing disunities? Was the presence of an abundant supply of labor in one area and a shortage in another significant in creating different reactions? Did climate and physical environment give a unique direction to colonial life in each empire? How important was the Indian problem? Hopefully, the selections included here will stimulate the search for answers and provide a broader framework for understanding the American colonial past.

A GENERAL DESCRIPTION
OF COLONIAL AMERICA

A General Description of America

EDMUND BURKE

Edmund Burke (1729-1797), English writer, orator, and politician, is known more for his opposition to British policy in America after 1763 and his distaste for the French Revolution than for the book on America from which this short selection has been taken. Published first in 1757, this work was highly popular in England and went through a number of editions. A careful observer and a persuasive writer, Burke was able to capitalize on the passionate interest of Europeans in things American by providing a colorful account of American history in its broadest sense. Primarily descriptive and narrative, Burke's work ranged over the colonial scene from Hudson Bay to Tierra del Fuego.

From Edmund Burke, *An Account of the European Settlements in America*, 5th ed. London: J. Dodsley, 1770, Vol. I, 203-208.

HAVING DESCRIBED, WITH AS MUCH CONCISENESS AS THE SUBJECT would bear, the manners of the original inhabitants of America, as we had before that related the most remarkable adventures of its discoverers and conquerors; it will be necessary to view more minutely, what and how advantageous a country these conquests and discoveries have added to the world; and what are the views, interests, and characters of those who at present possess the greatest part of that extensive region.

America extends from the North pole to the fifty-seventh degree of South latitude; it is upwards of eight thousand miles in length; it sees both hemispheres; it has two summers and a double winter; it enjoys all the variety of climates which the earth affords; it is washed by the two great oceans. To the Eastward it has the Atlantic ocean, which divides it from Europe and Africa. To the West it has another ocean, the great South Sea by which it is disjoined from Asia. By these seas it may, and does, carry on a direct commerce with the other three parts of the world. It is composed of two vast continents, one on the North, the other upon the South, which are joined by the great kingdom of Mexico, which forms a fort or isthmus, fifteen hundred miles long, and in one part, at Darien, so extremely narrow, as to make the communication between the two oceans by no means difficult. In the great gulph, which is formed between this isthmus and the Northern and Southern continents, lie an infinite multitude of islands, many of them large, most of them fertile, and capable of being cultivated to very great advantage.

America in general is not a mountainous country, yet it has the greatest mountains in the world. The Andes, or Cordilleras, run from North to South along the coast of the Pacific ocean. Though for the most part within the torrid zone, they are perpetually covered with snow, and in their bowels contain inexhaustible treasures. In the province of St. Martha[1] in South America are likewise very great mountains, which communicate with the former. In North America we know of none considerable, but that long ridge which lies to the back of our settlements, which we call the Apalachian, or Allegeney mountains; if that may be at all considered as a mountain, which upon one side indeed has a very great declivity, but upon the other is nearly on a level with the rest of the country.

Without comparison, America is that part of the world which is the best watered; and that not only for the support of life, but for the convenience of trade, and the intercourse of each part with the others. In North America the great river Missisippi, rising from unknown sources,

---

[1] Ed. NOTE: That portion of northern South America which includes Colombia and Venezuela.

runs an immense course from North to South, and receives the vast tribute of the Ohio, the Oubache,[2] and other immense rivers, scarcely to be postponed to the Rhine, or the Danube, navigable almost to their very sources, and laying open the inmost recesses of this continent. Near the heads of these are five great lakes, or rather seas of fresh water, communicating with each other, and all with the main ocean, by the river St. Laurence, which passes through them. These afford such an inlet for commerce as must produce the greatest advantages, whenever the country adjacent shall come to be fully inhabited, and by an industrious and civilized people. The Eastern side of North America which is our portion, besides the noble rivers Hudson, Delaware, Susquehanna, Patowmack, supplies several others of great depth, length, and commodious navigation. Many parts of our settlements are so intersected with navigable rivers and creeks, that the planters may be said, without exaggeration, to have each a harbour at his own door.

South America is, if possible, in this respect, even more fortunate. It supplies much the two largest rivers in the world, the river of Amazons, and the Rio de la Plata. The first, rising in Peru, not far from the South-Sea, passes from West to East, almost quite through the continent of South America, navigable for some sort or other of vessels all the way, and receiving into its bosom a prodigious number of rivers, all navigable in the same manner, and so great, that Monsieur Condamine[3] found it often almost impossible to determine which was the main channel. The Rio de la Plata, rising in the heart of the country, shapes its course to the South-East, and pours such an immense flood into the sea, that it makes it taste fresh a great many leagues from the shore; to say nothing of the Oronoquo, which might rank the foremost amongst any but the American rivers. The soil and products, in such a variety of climates, cannot satisfactorily be treated of in a general description; we shall, in their places, consider them particularly.

All America is in the hands of four nations. The Spaniards, who, as they first discovered it, have the largest and richest share. All that part of North America, which composes the Isthmus of Mexico, and what lies beyond that towards the river Missisippi on the East, the Pacific ocean to the West and North-west; and they possess all South-America excepting Brasil, which lies between the mouth of the river of Amazons and that of Plata along the Atlantic ocean; this belongs to Portugal. That part of North America which the Spaniards have not, is divided between

[2] ED. NOTE: The Missouri River.

[3] ED. NOTE: Charles Marie de la Condamine (1701-1774) was leader of an expedition to Ecuador in 1735 which attempted to determine the exact length of a degree at the equator.

the English and French. The English have all the countries which incircle Hudson's Bay, and thence in a line all along the Eastern shore to the thirtieth degree of North latitude. France claims the country which lies between this and the Spanish settlements to the West, and secures an intercourse with them by the mouths of the Missisippi, the Mobile, and of the river St. Laurence, which are the only avenues of navigation to this very extensive country. The multitude of Islands, which lie between the two continents, are divided amongst the Spaniards, French, and English. The Dutch possess three or four small islands, which, in any other hands, would be of no consequence. The Danes have one or two; but they hardly deserve to be named amongst the proprietors of America.

THE CONCEPT OF EMPIRE
IN COLONIAL AMERICA

Spain and the Conquest of Utopia

ERIC WOLF

Eric Wolf's book, *Sons of the Shaking Earth,* traces the development of Middle America—primarily Mexico and Guatemala—from pre-Columbian times to the present. A professor of anthropology at the University of Michigan, Wolf naturally stresses society, culture, and changes in the Indians' cultural milieu. But his wide-angled narrative also encompasses many other historical strands, and in the following selection he explores the motives and mystique of the Spanish conquerors—soldiers, functionaries, and friars.

"Their purpose had a transcendental simplicity; gold, subjects, souls."

Reprinted from *Sons of the Shaking Earth* by Eric Wolf by permission of The University of Chicago Press. Chicago, 1959, pp. 152-175. Copyright © 1959 by The University of Chicago.

Wolf observes at one point. This simple sentence captures the theme explored in the first section of this book. Reduced to such terms, all three imperial powers had much the same motives and, as Wolf warns, it is well to bear this in mind instead of accepting old preconceptions about Spanish and French selfishness, authoritarianism, and bigotry. But the student of comparative history must go further in his questioning: How did the three searches for wealth differ? What kinds of subjects—native and European—did the European states desire? What form did the religious motive take? As Wolf indicates, accidents of Spanish history and conditions in areas conquered by Spain profoundly affected the answers to these questions.

The reader may wish to speculate about the consequences for Spanish and American history had Columbus been delayed until Spain, following up the expulsion of the Moors, had pursued them into their African lands. He may wonder also if the later French and British imperial builders borrowed, in any sense, their motives and drives from their Spanish predecessors. He may ask what forces drove hundreds of thousands of Spaniards to follow the trail of the conquistadores to the New World, a subject which Irving Leonard touches upon in a later selection. But these are not Wolf's concern in this passage, as he describes the most significant components of the Spanish drive to empire.

IN 1492, CHRISTOPHER COLUMBUS, SAILING UNDER THE FLAG OF Castile, discovered the islands of the Caribbean and planted upon their shores the standard of his sovereigns and the cross of his Savior. From these islands, the newcomers began to probe the Middle American coast. In Easter week, 1519, a young adventurer, Hernán Cortés—lawyer by professional training and military man through baptism of fire on Santo Domingo—landed in the vicinity of San Juan de Ulua in Veracruz. He brought with him an army of 508 soldiers—32 of whom were crossbowmen and carried harquebuses—16 horses, and 14 pieces of artillery, together with a navy of 11 ships and 100 sailors. In July and August of that year, Cortés beached his ships and embarked on the conquest of Tenochtitlán. Two years later, on August 13, 1521, Tenochtitlán fell into Spanish hands. One cycle of history had come to an end and another cycle began.

How is one to explain this sudden irreversible change in the fate of Middle America? The entire enterprise of the Spanish Conquest seems shrouded in a curious air of unreality. Hernán Cortés conquers an empire embracing millions of people. For lack of holy water, a Fray Pedro de Gante baptizes hundreds of thousands of Indians with his saliva. A Núñez Cabeza de Vaca sets out to find the golden cities of Cíbola and the Fountain of Youth, to be shipwrecked, reduced to starvation, nearly eaten by cannibals, only to return to the fray as soon as he is rescued. Actors, acts, and motives seem superhuman: their lust for gold and for salvation, their undivided loyalty to a distant monarch, their courage in the face of a thousand obstacles seem to defy simple psychological explanations. They not only made history; they struck poses against the backdrop of history, conscious of their role as makers and shakers of this earth. The utterances of a Cortés, a Pánfilo Narváez, a Garay, are replete with references to Caesar, Pompey, and Hannibal. Cortés plays not only at being himself; he is also the Amadís of Gaul celebrated in the medieval books of chivalry. They were not satisfied with the simple act; they translated each act into a symbolic statement, an evocation of a superhuman purpose. Struck with admiration of their deeds and postures, their chroniclers took them at their word. In the pages of the history books these men parade in the guise of their own evaluation of themselves: half centaurs, pawing the ground with their hoofs and bellowing with voices like cannon, half gods, therefore, and only half men.

But their image of themselves obscures the real greatness of their achievement, for greatness can be measured only on a human scale, not on a divine. Part of their greatness was undoubtedly due to the military tactics employed by a courageous and cunning general. The Spaniards used cavalry to break through the massed formations of an enemy that had never before encountered horses; they thus avoided hand-to-hand combat in which gunpowder and iron arms would have been of little avail in the face of the wicked Indian swords, beset with obsidian chips. To counteract the Indian firepower of spears and arrows, the Spaniards used the crossbow, the instrument that gained them such a decisive victory in the great battle of Pavia against the remnants of French knighthood. When Spanish cavalry, artillery, and infantry proved impotent against Indian canoes manned by archers in the canals and lagoons surrounding Tenochtitlán, Cortés again carried the battle to the enemy, attacking the embattled capital across the water, from the boards of thirteen ships built on the spot.

None of these military successes would have been possible, however, without the Indian allies Cortés won in Middle America. From the first, he enlisted on his side rulers and peoples who had suffered grievously at the hands of their Mexica[1] enemies. In a decisive way, as Ralph Beals has put it, "the conquest of Tenochtitlán was less a conquest than it was a revolt of dominated peoples." Spanish firepower and cavalry would have been impotent against the Mexica armies without the Tlaxcaltec, Texcocans and others who joined the Spanish cause. They furnished the

---

[1] ED. NOTE: Professor Wolf prefers the term *Mexica* as more accurate than the more commonly used, *Aztec*.

bulk of the infantry and manned the canoes that covered the advance of the brigantines across the lagoon of Tenochtitlán. They provided, transported, and prepared the food supplies needed to sustain an army in the field. They maintained lines of communication between coast and highland, and they policed occupied and pacified areas. They supplied the raw materials and muscular energy for the construction of the ships that decided the siege of the Mexica capital. Spanish military equipment and tactics carried the day, but Indian assistance determined the outcome of the war.

In an ultimate sense, the time was ripe for a redress in the balance of power in Middle America. Even Moctezuma, in his abode at Tenochtitlán, must have felt this, for we can read in his hesitations, in his hearkening to omens of doom, evidence of the doubt and uncertainty which was gnawing at the vitals of Mexica domination. The Spaniards provided the indispensable additional energy required to reverse the dominant political trend. Yet they were not mere agents of the indigenous will, mere leaders of an indigenous revolt. Cortés' genius lay precisely in his ability to play this role, to surround himself with charisma in the eyes of the Indians. Cortés played this role to the hilt, but with calculated duplicity. For the Spaniards had not come to Middle America to restore an indigenous society. They acted from autonomous motives which were not those of their Indian allies. Accepting the command of a people deeply accustomed to obedience through long participation in a hierarchical social order, they began to enact their own purposes, to realize their own ends, which were those of Spanish society and therefore alien and hostile to those of the Indians among whom they had begun to move.

To understand these ends, we must try to understand Spanish society of that time, a task in which we moderns experience a particular difficulty. The reduced and impoverished Spain of today obscures our understanding of the once wealthy and powerful empire upon which the sun never set. All too often, we tend to interpret the past by reconstructing it in the image of the present. Again, too often, we view Spain through the lens of a powerful political mythology, a mythology forged both consciously and unconsciously in Protestant countries to advance the liberating cause of Protestantism and republican institutions against Catholicism and monarchial absolutism. According to this mythology, a singularly partisan deity ranged himself on the side of human freedom and economic progress against "feudal" Spain. While in northern Europe right-thinking and industrious men put their shoulders to the wheel of the Industrial Revolution, the Catholic South remained sunk in medieval sloth. But the rise and decline of a society is not explained by recourse to political demonology; the truth is at once simpler and more complex.

Let us not forget that the Mediterranean and not the European North is the homeland of capitalism and of the Industrial Revolution. Italy, southern France, Spain, and southern Germany witnessed the rise of the first factories, the first banks, the first great fairs. At the time of the discovery of America, the Iberian Peninsula harbored thriving cities, humming with expanding wealth and trade. The sources of this prosperity were manifold: the sale of wool to England or to Flanders; the sale of iron wares to the Levant; the seizure and sale of slaves from the African coast; the quick raid on a Saracen stronghold or a pirate's lair. These were enterprises which demanded the utmost in individual stamina and personal valor; they were also exceedingly profitable. And in response the culture which fed upon an extension of these enterprises elaborated its peculiar image of the manly ideal; the overweening personality possessed of skill and courage. This ideal belonged as much to the medieval past as to the commercial future. It was inherently contradictory and revealed in its contradiction the opposing forces at work within the social system that gave it birth. Its heroes act; but the culture forms of their acts are not only rich in the symbolic pageantry of the medieval knight-crusader but also supreme examples of the exaltation of Renaissance man pioneering on new frontiers of thought and human behavior. Covertly, more than once, the goal of the act is profit, conceived as personal enhancement through the acquisition of gold and riches.

There were in reality two Spains, or two tendencies at work in the Iberian Peninsula. The first tendency was aristocratic, oriented toward warfare and the gain of riches by warfare. It was exemplified most clearly by the armies of Castile, composed of a warlike nobility and a warlike peasantry. These armies had been forged in the fight against the Moors, first in raid and counterraid, later in the systematic reconquest of the Moorish southland. The nobility, partly organized into religious orders of monastic warriors, saw in warfare a ready source of ego enhancement and looted wealth. Its traditional economic interest lay in the extension of grazing range for its herds of cattle and sheep, coupled with a flourishing export trade in wool to northern Europe. The peasantry, on the other hand, consisted of soldier-cultivators, recruited into the army by promises and guaranties of freedom from servile encumbrances and charters of local self-rule. These peasants desired land, free land, to divide among their sons. In warfare, both nobility and peasantry gained their divergent ends.

The other Spain, the other Spanish trend, was less involved in warfare; it pointed toward capital accumulation through rising industry and trade in the hands of a town-based bourgeoisie. Such entrepreneurs existed in all Peninsular towns; but only in eastern Spain, centered in Catalonia, had they gained sufficient power to check the expansionist desires of the aristocratic soldiery. In this part of Spain, a bloody peasant war had smashed the remnants of a feudal system of the classic European kind. Traditional relationships in which a lord exercised economic, judicial, and social control of a group of serfs had given way to new social ties. A free peasantry populated the countryside; a prosperous bourgeoisie, long oriented toward maritime trade, controlled the towns. The country was undergoing incipient industrialization and the cloth, leather, and iron wares so produced were exchanged in the eastern Mediterranean for the drugs, dyestuffs, and luxury goods of the Orient.

By 1492, these two Spains were headed for collision, a conflict which might well have altered the face of Spain but for the discovery of America. The fall of the last Moorish redoubt put an end to the limitless acquisition of land by conquest and to the easy accumulation of wealth by forceful seizure; 1492 marked the closing of the Spanish frontier. As land became scarce, interests which had run parallel up to that time began to conflict; while the soldier-peasant wanted unencumbered land, the aristocrat wanted open range for sheep and cattle or land for dependent cultivators. With the distribution of the fruits of conquest among the conquerors, moreover, readily available wealth became unavailable. How was new wealth to be produced? To this problem the merchant-entrepreneur of the towns had an answer: capital investment in industry coupled with the reduction of aristocratic power. At this moment, however, the doors to the New World swung wide open to reveal a new frontier: dream cities of gold, endless expanses of land, huge reservoirs of dependent labor. The merchant-entrepreneur receded into obscurity; the knight-adventurer, the visionary of wealth through seizure at sword's point, gained new impetus.

It was this new frontier which settled the fate of Spain. Paradoxically, Spanish industry was to be swamped in a tide of gold from the Indies, which spelled its ultimate ruin; paradoxically, also, the new frontier destroyed the class which might have carried such industrialization to a successful conclusion. For in this New World, all men—peasant, merchant, impoverished noble, noble merchant-prince—could dream of becoming lords of land, Indians, and gold. Men who in Spain might have allied themselves politically and economically with the entrepreneurs and traders of the towns against the aristocrat could in this new venture identify themselves with the ideal of the mounted noble. Men who in Spain might have spurred the growth of the middle classes were here converted into its opponents. The year 1492 might have marked Spain's awakening to a new reality; instead, it marked the coming of a new dream, a new utopia.

Where men of varied pasts and varied interests engaged in a common enterprise, belief in a universal utopia renders possible their common action. Utopia asks no questions of reality; it serves to bind men in the service of a dream. Belief in it postpones the day of reckoning on which the spoils will be divided and men will draw their swords to validate their personal utopia against the counterclaims of their comrades-in-arms. Some came to the New World to find gold; others to find order, still others to save their souls. Yet in their common dream they asked no questions of one another. For the time being, their dream was validated by their common experience on board ship, by their common sufferings in the face of the enemy, by their common victory.

In the course of their common adventure in utopia they also achieved a set of common usages and understandings which made "the culture of the Conquest" different from their ancestral culture and from the culture still to be in the New World. Their purposes had a transcendental simplicity; gold, subjects, souls. This simplicity patterned their behavior and their thought, some of it conscious, self-imposed. The colonist-to-be in search of his liberty casts off the traditional forms which he has experienced as shackles and encumbrances. The royal official in search of order abhors the tangle of inherited forms of the Old World. The friar leaves behind him a world which is old and corrupt; in utopia he seeks austerity and clarity. The very process of migration produces a simplified stock of cultural forms.

Men drawn from all walks of life, the conquerors were not a complete sample of their ancestral society. They did not bring with them complete knowledge of the gamut of Spanish culture. Some of this age-old heritage they could not reproduce in the New World because they lacked acquaintance with it. Some of it, however, vanished in the crucible of their common experience, in their need to develop a common cultural denominator, to facilitate their common task. Spain, but recently unified under one crown, had remained a cultural plural, a mosaic of many parts. Yet the culture of the conquerors was, by contrast, highly homogeneous. This simplification extended to material goods: only one plow, of the many Spanish plows, was transmitted to the New World; only a few techniques of fishing were selected from the plethora of Spanish fishing techniques and transplanted into the new setting. Simplification extended also to symbolic behavior: speech undergoes a leveling, a planing-down of the formalities of Castilian Spanish into a plain and utilitarian idiom. Left behind are the many Spanish folk fiestas in honor of a multitude of beloved local saints; they yield in the New World to the measured and standardized performance of the formal celebrations of way stations in the life of Christ. The culture of the conquest was, as George Foster has pointed out, *sui generis*. In vain one looks in the culture of these men for the rich varied regional heritage of the mother country.

Some of the conquerors wanted gold—gold, the actual tangible substance, not the intangible "promises to pay" of later capitalism. In this they were children of their times, caught in the contradiction between medieval magic and the modern search for profits. All over Europe men longed for gold, encountered gold in dreams, dug for it under trees and in caves, sold their souls to the devil for it, labored over retorts to obtain it from base metals such as iron or lead. It was a kind of illness, and Cortés stated it that way—half cynically and half realistically—in addressing the first Mexica noble he met; "The Spaniards are troubled with a disease of the heart for which gold is the specific remedy." The illness was greed, but beyond greed the desire for personal liberty, escape of the ego from bondage to other men, "spiritual autarchy," as Eliseo Vivas has said, "which is achieved only when you are able to say to another man, *a mi no me manda nadie*—no one bosses me; I am lord because I have land and Indians, and I need not beg any favors from you or any one else." This is the new self-made man talking, the medieval adventurer on the threshold of capitalism, knight-errant in cultural form but primitive capitalist in disguise. The goal is medieval—never again to bend one's will to that of another—but the instrument is modern: the instrument of wealth.

Utopia thus bears at the outset the mark of a contradiction, between the past and future, a contradiction never wholly overcome. The contradiction is most startlingly illuminated when the Spanish entrepreneur is compared with his contemporary English rival. "The Englishmen," says Salvador de Madariaga,[2]

though on the surface more self-seeking, were in depth more socially minded; the Spaniards, though in appearance more statesmanlike and creative, more intent on "ennobling" cities and setting up kingdoms, were more self-centered. The Englishman, with his dividends, socialized his adventures, gain, booty; the Spaniard, with his hospitals, foundations, cathedrals, colleges and marquisates, raised a monument to his own self.

The rise of puritanism in the Anglo-American world, so brilliantly analyzed by Max Weber and Richard Tawney, destroyed the contradiction between individual goals and cultural means. For in accepting the Protestant ethic of work and capital accumulation as virtue, the entrepreneur made himself an instrument of production, harnessed himself to the process of capital formation. In Anglo-America, the very means thus became the ends; in Ibero-America, means and ends remained at war

---

[2] ED. NOTE: A Spanish writer-historian-novelist-statesman whose books on colonial Hispanic America have made him one of the principal apologists for Spain in America.

with one another, contradictory, unresolved.

If some came in search of gold, and its promise of personal liberty, others came in search of order. Their deity was the absolute monarch; their religion the new religion of the reason of state. At the end of the fifteenth century the Spanish crown had just emerged victorious in its political battles against its rivals. With the help of the rising middle classes and the peasantry, it had successfully defeated the attempts of the aristocrats who wished to reduce the king once again to the passive position of a mere *primus inter pares*.[3] Yet this political success but threatened to put the king into the hands of the penny-wise merchants who wished to trade support for a veto over his military and bureaucratic expenditures. The long period of the reconquest had also brought with it a spate of *fueros* or local charters which exempted one or the other local or professional body from the application of the general law; many a king had traded local autonomy for support against the Moorish enemy.

In the conquest of the New World, the crown saw its opportunity to escape the limitations of internal Spanish politics. Gold from the Indies would enrich not only the eager adventurer; a fifth of all gold and silver mined in the New World would be the king's, to finance a royal army, navy, and officialdom, to build the bases of absolutist power upon institutions wholly independent of nobility, middle classes, or peasant cultivators. Wealth from the Indies would underwrite a state standing above all classes, above the endless quarrels of contending interest groups. This state would speak with a new voice, with a new will. It would no longer be bound by precedent; it would set aside solutions which had become traditional, overgrown with the "cake of custom" and with compromise. The New World would not have to grow, piecemeal, in the shadows of ancient complexities: it would be a planned world, projected into reality by the royal will and its executioners. Thus utopia would become law, and law utopian. If Spanish towns had been small, cramped within their rings of fortifications, crowded around small irregular squares, then the towns of the New World would be large, open, unfortified; built upon the gridiron plan; centered upon a spacious square dominated by church and city-hall as twin symbols of sacred and secular power; an architectural utopia conceived by Italian architect-dreamers and built in the New World by royal mandate.

Was it true that many Indians lived in scattered hamlets instead of stationary, circumscribed, concentrated settlements? Then let there be a law to force them to live in nucleated towns, each with its own church, each surrounded by its own fields—within a measure radius of 560 yards from the church steeple—so that they could learn to order their lives to

[3] ED. NOTE: First among peers.

the tolling of church bells and to the commands of royal officers. Land and people of utopia had both been conquered by the sword; but it would be the dry scratching of the goose-quill pen upon parchment that would turn utopia into reality. Let each Indian keep twelve chickens and six turkeys and sell them for no more than 4 reales per turkey and 1½ reales per chicken; let each Indian working in a textile mill receive a daily ration of eighteen tortillas or fourteen tamales, plus chili, chickpeas, and beans. No problem was too insignificant to demand solution, and all solutions were solutions of law. Utopia was to be born also with this fatal deficiency implicit in the contradiction of law and reality. Reality is too protean to be wholly covered by law; it soon grows through, around, and over law, leaving but a hollow shell of words, a gesture of etiquette to gloss over the gap between wish and existence. The Latin American world still bears this legacy of law as a gesture of initiate action, to create a new order, and—when the energy of the gesture is spent—to use the law as wish, to wipe out a reality grown beyond law and order, beyond utopia.

Utopia contained many houses. If some men longed for gold, to build upon it their untrammeled liberty, and if others sought Indian subjects to rule and exercise in the spirit of the new order, so there were men who came to save souls. Upon the ruins of pagan shrines and idols in a new continent filled with souls hungry for salvation, yet uncorrupted by the age-old vices of the Old World, they would erect their own utopia: the prelude on earth of the Kingdom of Heaven. To these prophets of salvation, the conquest of the New World was the call to a great spiritual task: the defeat of Satan in his own redoubt, the redemption of souls languishing in his power, the annunciation of the faith in the one true God. The shock troops of this new faith were the friars, members of the monastic orders, strongly influenced by the reformist religious currents of the times. In some countries, such movements were soon to feed the flames of the Protestant revolution. If this did not happen in Spain, it was not because Spain lacked inflammable intellectual tinder. The economic and political development of the country had given strong impetus to men who began to question long-accepted opinions and to explore new interpretations of Catholicism. Most of these questioners were influenced by Erasmus of Rotterdam (1466-1536), whose teaching deemphasized the importance of formal ritual and stressed the promptings to piety of an "inner" voice, and by the utopian and reformist thought of Thomas More (1478-1535) and Luis Vives (1492-1540).

The reason that this new religious current did not explode into open rebellion against accepted religious forms is to be found in the character of the Spanish state and the circumstances which surrounded it rather than in the intellectual heterodoxy of the movement. The Spanish state had no need to break with the papacy: it dictated ecclesiastical appointments in its own territory; it possessed the right to read and suppress papal bulls before making them public; it controlled the office of Inquisition; it even sponsored autonomy in doctrinal matters through its support of the belief in the immaculate conception of the Virgin Mary, long before this belief became official church dogma at the Council of Trent (1545-63). In other European states the hunger for land and capital was one of the chief underlying motives for religious reformation; after the break with Rome, the estates of the Church were divided among the members of the Protestant faction. In Spain, the frontiers had not yet closed. Until 1492 land and wealth were still to be had by fighting the Moors in southern Spain in the name of religion, and that year witnessed the opening of the new frontier in the New World, with its promise of gold and glory for all takers.

Under Cardinal Ximénez de Cisneros,[4] the Erasmists received royal approval. The crown saw in their effort to restore the simplicity and austerity of primitive Christianity—in the face of decay and corruption—a spiritual counterpart to its own efforts to centralize Spain and to endow the new empire with a unified sense of mission. Many of the friars who came to the New World had taken part in this religious renewal. The first twelve friars to set foot in New Spain -the so-called Apostolic Twelve—had all worked to spread the gospel of primitive Christendom in southern Spain. Fray Juan de Zumárraga (1461?-1548), the first archbishop of Mexico, was a follower of Erasmus and familiar with the utopian writings of Sir Thomas More. Vasco de Quiroga (1470-1565), the first bishop of Michoacán, actually established a replica of Sir Thomas More's Utopia among the Indian communities of his bishopric. All these soldiers of the faith favored poverty over wealth, communal property over private property. Carefully they labored to purge Catholicism of the accumulation of ritual, selecting from the profusion of religious ritual only the major ceremonials celebrating the way-stations of Christ's life. This desire for purity and simplicity they also expressed in their great single-naved churches, symbolic of the homogeneity of primitive Christian worship, uncluttered by devotion to smaller altars and lateral naves.

The utopia of gold and liberty crumbled in the tension between exaltation of the self, through valiant deeds, and wealth, the instrument selected for their validation. The utopia of order remained arrested in the legal gesture, attempting to stem the tide of real behavior. The utopia of

[4] ED. NOTE: The Cardinal-Regent of Spain after the death of King Ferdinand in 1516 and Inquisitor General of Spain from 1507 to 1517.

faith, too, was to founder, hoped-for morality all too often impotent in the face of stubborn secular demand. And yet, conversion proved a success. The romanticists have long delighted in discovering the idols behind altars, the Gods of the Cave transformed into Christs hanging upon the Cross, the earth goddesses disguised as Catholic Virgins, the braziers burning copal gum on the steps of the churches, and other evidences of pre-Conquest heritage in the religious beliefs and practices of modern Indians. There is much that is Indian in the Catholicism of Middle America; but more surprising than the numerous survivals of pre-Conquest ideas and rituals is the organizational success of the Catholic utopia in a country of different religions and languages. Wherever you go in Middle America, you encounter the images of the Catholic saints and the churches built by the conquerors. Christ and the Virgin may have been transmuted by the adoration of men who had worshipped the Sun and the Moon and the Earth and the Lords of the Four Directions; but when an Indians speaks of a human being today, he does not say "a man"; he says "a Christian," a believer.

How is this success to be explained? It is easy to dismember men with cannons; it is more difficult to tame their minds. Certainly military defeat played a part, because it provided a visible demonstration of the impotence and decadence of the Mexica gods. The Children of the Sun had died by the sword as they had lived by the sword. The old gods had failed. When the Spaniards had demanded that the Totonac of Cempoala destroy their idols, the people had recoiled in horror; yet when the conquerors hurled the idols to the ground and broke them to pieces, the idols had remained mute and defenseless. They had not smitten the foreigners; they had failed to show the power that was in them. When the priests released the stones from the Pyramid of Cholula which held back the magic water that was in the mountain so that it would drown the strange men in a flood, the channel remained dry, and their magic deserted them. When the Children of the Sun, the Toltec rulers of Tenochtitlán, called down the wrath of their terrible idol Hummingbird-on-the-Left upon their enemies, Hummingbird-on-the-Left remained silent. The mutilated idols of their gods now rested on the bottom of the lake from which they had set out to conquer the universe for the sun; and the rubble of their temples served as fill for the new city of Mexico which was to arise upon these ruins. The old gods were dead, and powerless.

Not that these old gods had been so greatly loved. We know—or we can guess—that the will of these gods and the burden of human sacrifice rested heavily upon the land. Worship of warrior gods and human sacrifice were religious activities consonant with the military character of Mexica expansion. Inevitably, however, peace and political consolidation brought to the fore alternative religious explanations of a less militaristic character. Quetzalcoatl,[5] the Shining Serpent, served as a symbolic form through which these new interpretations and longings could find expression. His latter-day attributes as a harbinger of peaceful productivity and human wisdom bear surprising similarity to the ideological dictates of Christianity. Indeed, the Spanish friars came to believe that Quetzalcoatl had been none other than the apostle Thomas, come to the New World to convert the Indians. The longing for peace and for an end to bloodshed provided a fertile soil for the diffusion of the Christian message.

Both religions, moreover, believed in a structured and ordered supernatural world, in which more powerful, unseen, and unfathomable divinities stood above local supernatural mediators of lesser scope and power that were yet more immediately tangible. The Middle American peasant, like his Spanish counterpart, focused his religious interest on these lowlier supernatural helpers. He was more interested in the powers that affected his crops, his children, his family, and the people with whom he was in immediate and personal contact, than in the ultimate powers and their manifestations, which absorbed the interest of the religious specialist. Among the gods of a multi-headed pantheon, his daily concern was with the gods of the earth, fertility, rain and water, with illness, with the immediate short-range future, with the malevolence of his neighbors. Where the Spanish peasant worshipped wooden saints, the Middle American peasant worshipped clay idols; both had recourse to the magical practices of folk medicine; both had a strong sense of omens; and both believed in the reality of witches who could be ordinary everyday people during the day and malevolent spirits in animal disguise at night.

The priests, the specialists of both religions, on the other hand, were the heirs of rich and complex intellectual traditions, trained in the esoteric interpretation of religious symbols whether these symbols concerned multiple incarnations of Tezcatlipoca or the implications of the Revelation of St. John the Divine. The concern of the priest was not the concern of the peasant, and yet the same religious structure could embrace both. As long as the priests remained in command, as ultimate mediators between gods and men and ultimate interpreters of this relationship, men could adapt the manifold religious patterns to suit their personal and local concerns. What was true of religious concerns also held true of gods. A god could be one or triune, unique or multiple, and interpretation could stress his oneness at one time, his multiplicity at another. The Mexica pantheon had embraced many local gods, and the Mexica priesthood had labored to equate these gods with their own

---

[5] ED. NOTE: One of the most important of the Mexica gods with whom Hernán Cortés has sometimes been linked.

inherited deities or with one another. The Catholic Church had a similar tradition of flexibility. Just as the cloak of the Virgin hid many a local Persephone or Isis along the shores of the European Mediterranean, or as an Odin hanging himself from the tree of life became a Christ, so a Hummingbird-on-the-Left became a Spanish St. James riding down upon the heathens; a Tlaloc, a Christian Señor de Sacromonte; a God of the Cave, the Lord of Chalma; and Our Lady Spirit, the Virgin of Guadalupe.[6]

The Catholic Church drove out the priests of the old gods and manned the pivotal points of the religious hierarchy with men ordained in its own cult. It destroyed the old idols and put an end to human sacrifices, burned the sacred picture books and relegated to oblivion much of the calendric and divinatory knowledge of its predecessors; but it also offered the common man a way in which he could cast his traditional attachments into new forms. The Catholic Church, like the solar religion of the Mexica rigid at the heights of command but flexible on the level of peasant household, built a bridge from the old order to the new. As Frank Tannebaum has said, "It gave the Indian an opportunity . . . to save his faith in his own gods."

This transition from the old to the new was eased also by an astonishing similarity in ritual and symbol between the old and the new religion. A Nahua or an Otomí would hardly know what to make of a Spanish friar who, hampered by the language barrier, pointed first to the sky to indicate heaven and then to earth to indicate hell, as a first lesson in Catholic catechism. But rituals can be observed and learned by imitation. Both religious traditions had a rite of baptism. In Catholicism, the child was baptized and named, thus including him among the true believers. The Mexica similarly bathed and named the child in a religious rite, and the Maya celebrated with a ceremony the first time the child was carried astride the hip. Both religious traditions had a kind of confession. The Mexica and the inhabitants of the Gulf coast confessed their sexual transgressions to a priest of the earth goddess Filth-Eater; the Zapotec had annual public confessions; and the Maya confessed themselves either to priests or members of their families in case of illness. Both religious traditions possessed a ritual of communion. The Catholics drank wine and swallowed a wafer to symbolize their contact with the divine blood and body of Christ; the Mexica consumed images of the gods made of amaranth and liberally anointed with sacrificial blood. Both people used incense in their churches; both fasted and did penance; both went on pilgrimages to holy places; both kept houses of celibate virgins. Both believed in the existence of a supernatural mother; and both believed in

[6] ED. NOTE: The patron saint of Mexico.

virgin birth. Where Catholics held that Mary conceived immaculately through the power of the Holy Spirit, the Mexica believed that their goddess Coatlícue had given birth to Hummingbird-on-the-Left, impregnated by an obsidian knife which fell from the sky. Both people made use of the cross. A white St. Andrew's Cross, representing the four directions of the universe, often graced the hat and shield of the Shining Serpent, and the Maya made frequent use of the symbol of the foliated cross. The Spaniards represented their sacred stories in passion plays; the Middle Americans represented the annual changes of vegetation and activities in their sacrifices.

The Catholic missionaries well recognized the danger which lay in the maintenance of similar outward forms of ritual upon conversion. Yet they were themselves unable to decide whether these similarities were merely the work of Satan laboring to duplicate in his hellish church the rituals of the church sanctified by God, or whether they might not indeed represent the precipitate of some previous Christian teaching, brought to the New World perhaps by no less a personage than the apostle Thomas. Whatever their doubts, the formal similarities between the two religious traditions permitted an easy transition for the worshipper and gave him continuity precisely in the realm in which continuity was vital: the realm of religious behavior.

Nor did the psychology of Spanish Catholicism differ greatly from the psychology of the Mesoamerican solar cult. The Spanish ideal of the austere knight, defending his honor and the Virgin against Moors or other unbelievers, was not far removed from the Mexica ideal of the jaguar-eagle knight, whose obsidian sword insured victory and sacrificial victims for the hungry deities of war. In both religions cruelty against others in warfare and exalted pride went hand in hand with sacrificial penance—cruelty against the self, performed by a Spanish conqueror in a hairshirt, by a Mexica noble torturing his flesh with sharp spikes of the century plant.

True to their hierarchical habits, the Spaniards expended their greatest religious effort in converting the nobles, who became their first converts, partly because of the similarity of motivation, partly because of a desire to achieve a secure place in the new Spanish hierarchy through baptism and Christian vows. At Tlaxcala, the first center of the Spanish missionary effort, the local aristocracy strove mightily to reserve for itself a monopoly of all new religious offices, even those of cook, janitor, and gardener in the new monasteries. Their children were the first beneficiaries of Spanish ecclesiastical schooling. They used their power to set the feet of their own tributaries upon the new road to salvation; these tributaries thus came to church, as Fray Mendieta said, "more for the sake of outer appearance, to follow the orders of the *principales* who wanted to deceive them than to find a remedy for their souls." With the nobles firmly dedicated to the worship of the new religion, the commoners could be converted in mass, often with no more than a token understanding of the new divinities they were to worship. Pedro de Gante, exemplary Franciscan and kinsman of Charles V, baptized Indians in Mexico City at a daily rate of 14,000.

To the task of mass conversion, moreover, the church brought an exemplary table of organization. Like the Middle American religion, it drew a line between religious specialists and lay worshippers. In both traditions, the priests were the final spokesmen of the divine realm, in contact with a world to which ordinary men had no access. In both religions, long training was required to make a man worthy of his special role, and in both religions, fasts, penances, self-torture, and sexual abstinence were required of priests to maintain their spiritual worth in the sight of the divine powers. Throughout the exercise of their spiritual role on earth, dress, residence, speech, and comportment marked them off from ordinary men. Such parallelism again eased the transition from the worship of the old gods to the worship of the new, maintaining as it did the hierarchy of channels through which supernatural commands were passed down to the lay believer.

To be sure, the Catholic Church was organized internally to take maximum advantage of the opportunities so offered. Its division into holy orders and secular clergy made for great flexibility in a situation where an advance guard was needed to establish new beachheads of the faith, while a rear-guard took over and consolidated the gains. The friars were the advance guard; the abiding missionary work of the sixteenth century which laid the basis for all later religious efforts was probably carried out by no more than one thousand individuals. Established in fortified churches within the core areas of the newly won land, they spread out in "missions of penetration" into areas where Spanish political control was often still in doubt, sometimes ahead of Spanish armies, sometimes in their wake. Always they linked these outposts with their home bases through "liaison missions," to which they could retreat or where they could seek new strength to carry on their task of penetration. The secular clergy, the ordinary priesthood, carried out the work of consolidation.

Inevitably there were quarrels and conflicts of jurisdiction as the work progressed, as well as conflicts of temperament. The holy orders recruited men whose personalities differed markedly from those characteristic of the regular clergy. The friars favored individuals who were more adventurous and utopian in outlook, as well as less amenable to routine and less adapted to the day-to-day life of a going society. The secular clergy showed more conservatism, less of a tendency to sacrifice reality to otherworldly visions and schemes. Thus the larger church benefited by its possession of both kinds of men, both kinds of organization. When the task of conversion was completed, the work of shepherding the flock through its daily tribulations could be turned over to men capable of preserving the gains.

The eventual adjustment of the religious dream to mundane reality was less than utopia, and yet it left an impress on the Indian population such as no other religious or political current has done to this day. Ultimately the message of salvation spelled hope for the Indian, not only hope in the transcendental realm of a supernatural life after death, but hope on earth, where utopia was yielding to the pressure of all too secular interests. Men would labor to deny him his humanity, to defend his use as a resource, a tool to be used and discarded at will; but against such claims of politicians, lawyers, and theologians, Pope Paul III would in 1537 assert, in his bull "Sublimis Deus":

The sublime God so loved the human race that he not only created man in such wise that he might participate in the good that other creatures enjoy, but also endowed him with capacity to attain to the inaccessible and invisible Supreme Good and behold it face to face [;] . . . all are capable of receiving the doctrines of the faith. . . . We . . . consider . . . that the Indians are truly men. . . .

To the Indian, the rite of baptism thus proved an assertion of his essential humanity, to be a man with human claims upon other men. Of this right no colonist or royal official could rob him. When the Indian re-emerges from beneath the wreckage of utopia, we find that he has rebuilt and cemented his new life with bonds drawn from the new religion, at once his opium, his consolation, and his hope of ultimate justice.

The Colonial Idea in England

HOWARD MUMFORD JONES

Without denying the importance of "gold, subjects, souls" as motives for empire, Howard Mumford Jones approaches them from a different angle. As professor of American literature at Harvard University and as a long-time student of intellectual life and culture, Jones has observed American history with the perceptive eye of the humanist. Emphasizing literary works as a reflection of ideas and attitudes, he has related the literature of an epoch to events and institutions within it.

This is a particularly useful technique in the present case, for British colonial expansion depended very heavily upon extra-governmental support which could be mobilized only by what we would today call "propaganda." Tudor and Stuart monarchs encouraged expansion by granting charters, monopolies, and privileges (and revoking them when it suited their purpose), and sometimes by investing capital. On the whole, however, colonization was carried on by private or semiprivate corporations, modeled after earlier trading enterprises, which gave impetus to expansion.

Some might argue that Jones overstresses the importance of the English experience with the Irish. Among other things they could point out that royal power was directly employed in the Emerald Isle, that native inhabitants could not (like the Indians in America) be driven westward out of the way, and that the institutions imposed upon Ireland were modeled as closely as possible after those in England itself. Still, the emphasis upon the negative effect of this venture in Ireland helps to explain why it took England so long to join the competition for empire in America, and to indicate the strength of the forces which ultimately overcame the barrier built up by the Irish precedent.

This selection brushes aside well-worn themes—the role of the religious rebel (in some cases Catholic, more often Puritan), the search for individual liberty—to stress the broad national forces at work in England. One of them—the desire to remove troublesome vagabonds and derelicts from the English scene—appears to have no counterpart in the Spanish experience. Others are similar to, but both subtly and significantly different in shading from, those which Eric Wolf has spelled out.

A S TIME DRIFTED ON, THE MIST OF UNCERTAINTY THAT SHROUDED South America, the Caribbean, and North America in a vague blur known as the Indies or the New World slowly lifted; and when the outlines of the North American continent became clearer to English seamen and to Tudor and Stuart monarchs, a colonial impulse began to stir. Before passing to this specific theme, however, it is well to be reminded of a profound difference between the concept of imperial expansion under the Spanish crown and the curious and tentative beginnings, half private, half official, of English expansion overseas to the New World. In the Caribbean and on the Spanish Main the dynamism of royal power found its center in the municipality, or *cabildo,* a semi-autonomous unit partly medieval in political structure, striving to be a city, and often in fact becoming one, as the history of Santo Domingo, Havana, Panama, and Vera Cruz demonstrates. The *cabildo,* under the crown, possessed or directed administrative, judicial, and military powers and activities, served as a base for further conquest, and was a market for provincial trading and international wares, a collecting point for the king's revenue, and a center of religious authority, since it was commonly the seat of a bishop. This concept was alien to English experience. English settlements, tentative and timid on the Maine coast, or fumbling and ill-directed at Roanoke Island, Jamestown, or Cape Cod, were clearly not of this order. If one inquires why, when the Spanish were planting "colonies" at the end of the fifteenth century, the English waited until after the opening of the seventeenth to create colonies of their own, one is forced back upon important historical and political considerations.

The Tudor kings did not lack enterprise, but their hands were full, of necessity or design, with other problems. In the first place Henry VII had to consolidate his little kingdom, conciliate or repress dissatisfaction, and rescue his treasury from bankruptcy. In the second place Henry VIII was temperamentally more interested in the Field of the Cloth of Gold and in being a European power than he was in the cold wilderness of North America; and his political, matrimonial, and theological troubles were many and vexing. In the third place, until James I ascended the English throne, Scotland was a hostile power, the Welsh were commonly unbiddable, and the Irish would not be subdued. In the fourth place English foreign trade at the opening of the sixteenth century was largely in the hands of Mediterranean and Baltic merchants, and the process of repossessing that trade for English merchants and English shipping was long, arduous, and complex. In the fifth place there was a sheer lack of money and men, despite the cry of overpopulation, as any student of Elizabeth's tortuous policies, foreign and domestic, soon comes to realize; and when the English eventually found enough risk capital (to which the sale of the monasteries contributed), a steady income from the Muscovy trade was more attractive than wild and mutinous adventures on the shores of Newfoundland or up the Orinoco. In the sixth place the reports brought back by those who, like Frobisher and Davis, had sought a Northwest passage comparable to the Baltic were uninviting—so much so that a document such as Gilbert's *Discourse of a Discovery for a New Passage to Cataia* (1576) had to expand a good deal of rhetoric to prove that life in that part of the New World was not as bad as it had been painted. Finally, once the Protestant religion had been established and England found herself pitted against the most powerful Catholic power in the world, the sixteenth-century Caribbean offered a fine fusion of patriotism, plunder, and salvation, immensely appealing to mercantilist adventurers who thought of economic wealth principally in terms of bullion.

The terms customary in sixteenth and early seventeenth-century writing about overseas settlements were "colony" and "plantation." These were novel words. There is little or no evidence that English thought about colonization was influenced by Greek or Roman theory, which is not cited in the literature until late. Jamestown was of course a Stuart counterpart of a Greek colony in the Aristotelian sense that its inhabitants could be reached by the voice of a single herald, and it developed a military garrison vaguely like that of a Roman *colonia,* but the parallel is accidental. In Middle English the word "colonie," like its medieval Latin counterpart, referred to a settlement of agricultural laborers associated with a particular portion of the earth's surface, but this is not an appropriate term for Tudor settlements. English plantations in Ireland were not known as colonies. The earliest discoverable appearance of "colony" in the sense of a settlement in a new or foreign country politically dependent upon the parent state seems to be in a Scottish document of 1548-1549; its appearance in English proper is in Eden's translation of Peter Martyr in 1557. According to the *New English Dictionary,* Bacon in 1622 was the first to use the verb "to colonize." Even "plantation" in the sense of a foreign colony appears relatively late, the first recorded instance being in Hooker's *History of Ireland* (1558). The late appearance of these terms suggests that, despite the activity of the Spaniards, the Portuguese, and the French, English thinking about the nature of a colony had to begin virtually *de novo.*

There were nevertheless historical and foreign precedents that seem to have colored English thought. The Roman and the Scandinavian conquests of Britain, not to speak of the Norman conquest, furnished examples. Not only did Virginia and New England employ a warrior-settler type of occupier (as Pennsylvania, for example, did not), but propagandists recognized the validity of the historical appeal. Thus the Reverend William Crashaw in *A Sermon Preached in London before . . . his Maiesties Counsell for . . . Virginea, Febr. 21, 1609* (London, 1610) roundly urged that "stately houses, costly apparell, rich furniture, soft beds, daintie fare, dalliance and pleasures . . . are not the means whereby *our forefathers* conquered kingdomes, subdued their enemies, conuerted heathen, ciuilized the Barbarians, and setled their common-wealths." And William Strachey, in his "Praemonition to the Reader" in *The Historie of Travaile into Virginia Britannia* (written about 1613), is explicit about the Romans and the "Scots":

Had not this violence and this injury bene offred to us by the Romans (as the warlike Scots did the same, likewise, in Caledonia, unto the Picts), even by Julius Caesar himself, then by the emperour Claudius . . . who reduced the conquered partes of our barbarous iland into provinces, and established in them colonies of old souldiers . . . we might yet have lyved overgrowen satyrs, rude and untutred, wandring in the woodes, dwelling in caves, and hunting for our dynners, as the wild beasts in the forrests for their praye.

But all this is remote, rhetorical justification; what is more pertinent are the colonies of the Hanseatic cities in the Baltic and of the Italian city republics, notably Venice and Genoa, in the Levant. By establishing outposts in the Aegean islands, at Athens, in the Black Sea, in Egypt, and elsewhere, Venice, for example, founded trading posts or *fondachi.* Over them the influence of the metropolis was supreme. The original grant permitting their creation in a foreign country was obtained by the metropolis, buildings were erected at public cost, and magistrates were appointed by the home government. These magistrates were responsible in Venice to a body somewhat like the (later) English Board of Trade and Plantations. Venetian laws were carried into the *fondaco,* the trade of which was monopolized by the mother city. Associated with the creation and management of such a colony and its commerce was a joint-stock company, a fourteenth-century invention by which state action could be conveniently concealed as private enterprise.

Because of the prestige of Italian commercial theory in Renaissance Europe, and because trade relations between England and Venice were often close, the *fondaco* idea may fairly be said to have influenced Tudor thought about colonies. Like the *fondaco,* the English settlement was often the product of joint-stock enterprise chartered by the state (the crown). The governor, "admiral," and council (if there was one) were appointed by the crown, removable by the king, and expected to follow specific instructions from the home authorities. English law (or "rights") was usually carried into the settlement by express provision of charter or patent, colonial trade was monopolized by the mother country, and in their earlier years English settlements expected forts, storehouses, churches, and other public structures to be put up at government expense. Indeed, the treaties settlers made with Indian "kings" suggest the analogy of Venetian agreements with foreign powers. From the point of view of the crown the creation of a settlement that would send wealth home was an overriding consideration; and since risk capital in England was found in the cities, the cities, with the approbation of the crown, had their relations with the new project—as, for example, in the case of the "London Company." The first colonial administrators were at once military chiefs, ambassadors, judges, and commercial agents. In general this concept of planting a settlement explains the almost immediate development of conflict between the colonial "administration" dutifully enforcing the *fondaco* concept, and colonists primarily interested in the private ownership of land and in private profits.

II

More immediate, however, was the example of Ireland; and the struggles of sixteenth-century Englishmen to subdue the wild Irish and to strengthen imperial rule profoundly colored the concept of a plantation, influenced the appeal of "promotion" literature, and created certain important misconceptions about the New World.

Before the accession of Henry VIII, English power in Ireland had sunk to the lowest ebb in history. In rebuilding his empire Henry at first attempted conciliation as a means to draw the natives into civilized life that would benefit trade. But the Irish proved recalcitrant, a combination of conciliation with coercion seemed necessary, and only by the ruthless suppression of rebellion did Lord Grey manage to govern Ireland without undue bloodshed until 1540. After Henry's death disaffection became chronic and desolation spread. Though the English monopoly of gunpowder gave an overwhelming superiority to the royal forces, it became evident that mere military forays could not hold that country. If Ireland had never existed, the English in America would probably have refused to sell firearms to Indians who were "naked and unarmed, destitute of edged tools and weapons," but the immediacy with which English colonists were instructed to keep the natives unarmed suggests the pertinence of Irish experience. Of course the regulation was frequently violated.

The idea of English plantations in Ireland became even more prominent during the reign of Elizabeth. One may note that Irish anarchy carried with it three important corollaries. One was that the Irish service was unpopular. It was "well known to be the most miserable war for travail, toil and famine in the world," said one observer in 1598; and in 1599 Sir John Dowdall wrote Cecil that "most part of the army . . . seem beggarly ghosts, fitter for their graves than to fight a prince's battle. The report hereof so works in mens minds that they had as lief go to the gallows as to the Irish wars." The reasons for this unpopularity were many—bad pay, insufficient provisions, incompetent leadership—but a leading one was the character of Irish warfare. That warfare was compounded of ambush and treachery. The Irish, wrote Gainsford in *The Glory of England* (1618),

. . . will plash down whole trees over the passes, and so intricately wind them, or lay them, that they shall be a strong barricade, and then lurk in ambush amongst the standing wood, playing upon all comers as they intend to go along. On the bog they likewise presume with a naked celerity to come as near our foot and horse as is possible, and then fly off again, knowing we cannot or indeed dare not follow them.

The second result of Irish conflict was the desolation of the country. The island acquired the reputation of being a desert. Everyone is familiar with Spenser's description of the starving Irish, but Spenser's was not the only one. In 1575 Sir Henry Sidney wrote the Lords of the Council about Offaly and Leix, where English plantations had been attempted, that the land was "spoiled and wasted, by the race and offspring of the old native inhabitors, which grow great, and increase in number; and the English tenants decay, both in force and wealth. . . . They are daily so spoiled and burned, the charges they have been at, and their daily expenses they be at, to defend themselves, so weakeneth them, as their state is to be pitied." In 1598 Chief Justice Sir William Saxey said in a letter to Cecil that Munster had been left desolate by Irish rebels. He described "infants taken from the nurses' breasts, and the brains dashed against the walls; the heart plucked out of the body of the husband in the view of the wife, who was forced to yield the use of her apron to wipe off the blood from the murderer's fingers; [an] English gentleman at midday in town cruelly murdered, and his head cleft in divers pieces; divers sent into Youghal amongst the English, some with their throats cut, but not killed, some with their tongues cut out of their heads, others with their noses cut off." In 1599 an official minute declared that "we see by manifold experience, what madness it is for a Deputy or General to lead royal forces against naked rogues in woods and bogs, whom hounds can scarce follow, and much less men. Their ordinary food is a kind of grass. Neither clothes nor houses, generally, do they care for. With this their savage life are they able to wear out any army that seeketh to conquer them." The writer compares the wild Irish to wolves and foxes. And in Fynes Moryson's *Itinerary* (1617) one reads of "a most horrible specta- cle of three children . . . all eating and gnawing with their teeth the entrails of their dead mother . . . the common sort of the rebels were driven to unspeakable extremities." He reports that old women caught, killed, and ate little children.

It appeared that a race capable of these atrocities was little better than bestial. Said William Thomas in *The Pilgrim: A Dialogue on the Life and Actions of Henry VIII* (1552):

. . . the wild Irish, as unreasonable beasts, lived without any knowledge of God or good manners, in common of their goods, cattle, women, children and every other thing . . . nor yet any justice executed for murder, robbery, or other like mischief; but the more force had ever the more reason. And hereof it followed that because their savage and idle life could not be satisfied with the only fruit of the natural unlaboured earth, therefore continually they invaded the fertile possessions of their Irish neighbours that inhabited the . . . English Pale.

Sure, Sir Henry Sidney wrote the queen in 1567,

. . . there was never people that lived in more misery than they do, nor as it should seem of worse minds, for matrimony among them is no more re- garded in effect than conjunction between unreasonable beasts. Perjury, rob- bery, and murder counted allowable. . . . I cannot find that they make any conscience of sin, and I doubt whether they christen their children or no; for neither find I place where it should be done, nor any person able to instruct them in the rules of a Christian; or if they were taught I see no grace in them to follow it; and when they die I cannot see they make any account of the world to come.

Spenser returns to the ancient Scythians to find a parallel to Irish bar- barism:

There bee other sortes of cryes all so vsed amongst the Irishe, which savoure greatlie of *Scithian*: barbarisme, as theire Lamentacions at theire burialls, with disparefull outcryes and ymoderate waylinges . . . since I latelie spake of theire manner of cryes in ioyninge battaile, to speake also somewhate of the manner of theire Armes and arraye in Battaile . . . And first of theire armes and weapons, amongst which theire broade swordes are proper *Scithian:* . . . Also theire shorte bowes and little quivers with shorte bearded arrowes, are verie *Scythian*.
. . . Moreover theire longe broade shieldes, made but of wicker roddes which are commonlie vsed amongst thee . . . Northerne Irishe. . . . Likewise

theire going to battayle without Armour on their bodies or heades, but trusting onelie to the thickness of theire glibbs [matted hair over the eyes], the which they saye will sometymes beare of a good strooke, ys meere salvage and Scythian . . . besides theire confused kynde of march in heapes without any order or arraye, their Clashinge of swordes togeather, their fierce rvnninge vpon theire Enemies, and theire manner of feighte, resembleth altogeather that which is redd . . . to haue bene vsed of the Scythians.

. . . so haue I sene some of the Irishe [drink] not theire Enemies but frindes bloode, as namelie at the execution of a notable tratour. . . . I sawe an old woman . . . tooke vpp his heade whilst he was quartered and sucked vpp all the blood running there out sayinge that the earth was not worthie to drincke yt, and therewith also steeped her face and brest and tare her haire cyringe and shriking out most tirriblie.

The point is not the bias or inaccuracy of such reports; the point is that this picture of Ireland and the Irish preceded or accompanied the voyage literature having to do with the New World, that English experience with one wild race conditioned their expectation of experience with another, and that the deep popular disfavor into which Irish expeditions fell inevitably prejudiced colonial enterprise in North America.

For, point by point, these observations are paralleled in writing about the American Indians. Take the matter of ambush. The Jacobean reader of Hakluyt's translation of a narrative of the De Soto expedition, *Virginia Richly Valued* (1609), discovered that Indians are

. . . a people so warlike and so nimble, that they care not a whit for any footemen. For if their enemies charge them, they runne away, and if they turn their backs, they are presently upon them. . . . They never stand still, but are alwaies running and traversing from one place to another; by reason whereof neither crossebow nor arcubuse can aime at them; and before one crossebowman can make one shot, an Indian will discharge three or foure arrowes; and he seldom misseth what hee shooteth at.

Or he might read of the bloody treachery at Mavila, or the burning of De Soto's horses at Chicaca.

. . . for all their faire and cunning speeches, they are not overmuch to be trusted, for they be the greatest traitors of the world, as their manifold most craftie contrived and bloody treasons, here set down at large, doe evidently prove. They be also as unconstant as the wethercock, and most readie to take all occasions and advantages to doe mischiefe. They are great liars and dissemblers; for which faults oftentimes they had their deserved paiments. . . . To handle them gently . . . will be without comparison the best; but if gentle polishing will not serve, then we shall not want hammerours and rough masons enow, I meane our old soldiours trained up in the Netherlands.

This summary view of the Indians might be a discussion of the wild Irish.

If Spenser said the Irish scarcely knew the purpose of clothing, John Smith pictures the Indians "couered with the skinnes of wilde beasts," wearing "large mantels of deare skins not much differing in fashion from the Irish mantels," adorning themselves with "a dead Rat tied by the tail" or with live snakes that "often times familiarly would kiss [their] lips." The leggings of the New England savages reminded the author of *Mourt's Relation* of "Irish trouses," and Thomas Morton declared that the "Natives of New England are accustomed to build them houses much like the wild Irish." Spenser describes the Irish "cryes in ioyning battaile"; listen, now, to John Smith: "Vpon the first flight of arrowes, they gaue such horrible shouts and screeches, as though so many infernall helhounds could not haue made them more terrible." William Morrell in *Nova Anglia* could make Indian warfare clear only by comparing it to that of the Irish; and in 1637 Roger Williams, writing to John Winthrop, threatened that if the Indians were not kindly used, they might "turne wild Irish themselues." In sum, America was uncomfortably like Ireland.

A single instance will illuminate the unhappy parallel. Sir Humphrey Gilbert regularly put men, women, and children to the sword in Ireland; in Virginia Sir Thomas Dale dealt mercilessly with the Indians and all who consorted with them:

> Sr Tho: Dale haveinge allmoste finished the foarte, and settled a plantacyon in that p'te dyv^{rs} of his men being idell, and not willinge to take paynes, did runne away unto the Indyans; many of them beinge taken againe, Sr Thomas in a moste severe manner cawsed to be executed, some he appointed to be hanged, some burned, some to be broken on wheels, others to be staked, and some to be shott to deathe, all theis extreme and crewell tortures he used, and inflicted upon them, to terrefy the reste for attempteinge the lyke, and some wch robbed the store, he cawsed them to be bowned faste unto trees, and so starved them to deathe.

Indians bringing food were treated as spies: "Some of them Sr Tho: Gates cawsed to be apprehended and executed for a terrour to the reste, to cause them to desiste from their subtell practyses." Doubtless the Spaniards, the Portuguese, and the French were equally brutal in a cruel and brutal age, but the doctrine that the only good Indian is a dead Indian first took shape, it would appear, in the doctrine that the only good wild Irishman is a dead wild Irishman.

While Ireland was being terrorized into "civilitie," discharged soldiers, returning to England, filled the land with ill reports of Irish life, just as disgruntled sailors and settlers, returning from some ill-starred New

World venture, spread unfavorable reports about America. The two regions played into each other's hands. The misfortunes of the New World echoed the misfortunes of the Old; the situations were too much alike not to strengthen the assumption that colonial experience was everywhere of a piece. Unable to comprehend the Brehon laws, the English simply decided that the wild Irish were savages; unable to understand Indian "polity," they reached a like conclusion. Used to savagery in the one place, they looked for it, they provoked it, in the other.

III

The transfer of experience and ideas, expectation and emotional attitude from the struggle to "plant" Ireland to the endeavors toward colonizing North America was made easy by the fact that many of the leading proponents of American colonization, many of the "adventurers," and many of the actual leaders in New World ventures had had connections, sometimes unfortunate, with Irish affairs. Among the more famous names are those of Sir Humphrey Gilbert, Sir Walter Ralegh, Sir Francis Drake, Sir Ferdinando Gorges, the Earl of Southampton, Captain Ralph Lane, Lord De La Warr, Chief Justice Popham, Captain Christopher Carleill, and Lord George Carew, many of whom were also authors or instigators of influential "reports" on the New World. Sir Humphrey Gilbert had a military career in Ireland. After his raid on Nombre de Dios, Sir Francis Drake spent some time with Essex in Ireland, from which he emerged in 1575 to plan his circumnavigation of the globe. In January 1598/9 Sir Ferdinando Gorges was named sergeant-major of the army in Ireland; and though he seems not to have served, he must have learned something about Irish affairs. The Earl of Southampton went to Ireland in 1599 and again in 1600 on missions semi-military and semi-political, and during the parliamentary session of February-May 1624 he appeared as an authority on Irish affairs and was a member of the committee to consider the defense of that island. In the same epoch Lord De La Warr not only fought under Essex but was knighted by the Irish lord deputy. Gorges, Southampton, and De La Warr were of course, members of the Council of Virginia. Lord George Carew, a member both of the Council and of the Virginia Company, fought under Sir Henry Sidney in Ireland during the seventies, held a succession of important Irish posts in the eighties, and rose to even greater distinction in the Irish establishment at the close of the century. In 1603 he retired as Lord Justice for Ireland, but he revisited the country in 1610 to survey the Ulster settlements. Bacon's report to James I entitled "Certain Considerations Touching the Plantation in Ireland," dated 1606, praises Chief Justice Popham for his successes in the Munster plantations. Ralegh, of course, received a grant of 12,000 acres in Ireland and settled a large number of English families in Cork and Waterford about 1594. Ralph Lane was muster-master in Ireland in 1592 and submitted a project for musters in Ireland to the English authorities while he held that appointment. Captain Christopher Carleill served in Ireland in 1584 and again in 1588. Lord (formerly Captain) Chichester, another prominent Irish official, served with Carew on the committee to draw up a frame of government for Virginia. In general it can be demonstrated that a considerable number of the incorporators and "adventurers" of the original Virginia Company had an active interest in Irish plantations.

The doctrine that a plantation had to be, in its origins, a military establishment, and the excuse that native sloth made invasion and settlement necessary were, in addition to the misinterpretation of the "wild" inhabitants, the most important notions developed by the Irish experience and transferred to the New World. Equally important was the idea that the subjugation of, or through, a colony implied a system of feudal tenure. Having in mind the experience of over a century, Bacon thus proposed that the title of Earl of Ulster be added to that of the Prince of Wales, and that an Irish nobility be created, based on Irish landholding. He sketched a council in residence in Ireland and a council in London for governing the plantations. He argued likewise that there was no necessity for the undertakers to execute their duties in person, their kinsfolk, servants, and tenants sufficing, and said that settlement must take the form of towns. The parallels to early colonial theory regarding America are obvious. In the case of Nova Scotia, for example, Sir William Alexander in 1621 received a royal patent for all the land between New England and Newfoundland, and on the express analogy of the Ulster settlement of 1609 (which carried into effect Bacon's proposal of an Irish nobility) Alexander was authorized to set up the scheme of the Knights Baronets of Nova Scotia. For the sum of 300 "merks" (150 pounds sterling) any person approved by Sir William and the king might receive a patent of nobility of the Nova Scotia establishment, and 6000 acres of land. On this land it was his duty to establish settlements. One hundred thirteen such baronets were created, though most of them, through the payment of fines, were released from the necessity of providing settlers. Wars with France and the exchange of New World possessions between France and Great Britain stopped the operation of the scheme, but in making propaganda for his colony Alexander and his associate, Sir Robert Gordon of Lochinvar, addressed themselves mainly to the upper classes. Before one decides that so "aristocratic" a program sprang from the pedantry of James I, let him remember that it was in some such fashion that Ulster was subdued. Let him also recall the case of George Calvert, who owned 2300 acres of land in County Longford, became Lord Baltimore on the Irish establishment, was a member of the Virginia Company, acquired "Avalon" in Newfoundland, and asked for and received Maryland as a county palatine on terms his settlers later denounced as giving him more autocratic powers than were possessed even by the crown.

A succession of schemes, a program of propaganda for planting Englishmen on territory wrested from the wild Irish began as early as 1551. Anti-Irish gossip had to be offset by effective propaganda, the formula for which set the pattern of American "promotion literature." Thus *A Letter sent by the T. B. Gentleman unto his very frende Mayster R. C. Esquire, wherein is conteined a large discourse of the peopling and inhabiting the Cuntrie called the Ardes* (1572) not only outlines the mode of settlement that was to be tried at Jamestown, but anticipates many arguments concerning the New World. The climate and fertility of the country are praised, and private possession of land is promised. "How say you," inquires the author, "have I not set forth to you another Eutopia?" Prospective colonists are assured the land is empty and "lacketh only inhabitants, manurance, and pollicie." Three familiar themes appear: England was never so full of people,

. . . and the dissolution of Abbayes hath done two things of importance heerin. It hath doubled the number of gentlemen and marriages, whereby commeth daily more increase of people, and suche younger brothers as were wonte to be thruste into Abbayes, there to liue (an idle life), sith that is taken from them must nowe seeke some other place to liue in.

Again:

To inhabite and reforme so barbarous a nation as that is, and to bring them to the knowledge and law, were bothe a godly and commendable decde, and a sufficiet worke for our age. . . . Let us, therefore, vse the persuasions which Moses vsed to Israel, they will serue fitly in this place, and tell them that they shall goe to possesse a lande that floweth with milke and hony.

And finally

. . . it shall be furnished with a companie of Gentlemen and others that will liue frendly in felowships togither reioysing in the frute and commoditie of their former trauaile, which (through noble courage) for estimatiō sake, and the loue of their owne countrey the[y] first enterprised, deseruing . . . to be crowned with garlands of honours and euerlasting fame.

Unemployment and overpopulation, the missionary motive, and a union of profit and fame—experience taught the persuasive quality of these arguments.

In 1589 another characteristic pamphlet shows the deep unpopularity of the plantation-idea and the persistent desire to make emigration attractive through propaganda. Robert Payne in his *Brife description of Ireland* attempted to soften current prejudice against the wild Irish. He found the better sort of people "very ciuill and honestly giuen," said that most of the kerns and gallowglasses had been slain in the Desmond rebellion, and described the remaining Irish as harmless, idle folk like English beggars. They hated the Spaniards because of the Spaniards' "monsterous cruelties in the West Indians"—a note that is to recur in the American material. Ireland is incomparable; and he praises Irish forests, stone and mineral wealth, wild fowl, seafood, hunting, and agricultural plenty."You may keep a better house in Ireland for L. li, a yeere, then in England for CC.li. a yeere." The author admits there had been fraudulent men among previous "undertakers" in Ireland, who "enticed many honest men ouer, promising them much but performing nothing, no not so much as to pay their seruants, and workmen wages." But of course *his* undertakers, "many good knights and gentlemen of great worship," are worthy men. Much of the pamphlet seeks to allay popular fears. Any one of six million English, says the writer,

. . . is good innough for three wetherbeaten spainerds whom a fewe of our frostie nightes will make shrinke like rotten sheepe. yet thus much I must say for them, if almightie God for our contempt of his holye worde hath giuen them power against vs, as hee did the frogges against the Egiptianes, Then is there no force able to resiste them: (without that) I see no cause why we either in England or in Ireland should feare them.

Other documents on the Ulster "plantations" enumerate various "commodities" and do what they can to make emigration attractive; yet a survey of 1618-1619 showed only 1974 families in the six counties of Ulster, confessed to humiliating failure, and failed to foresee the success of the English plantations in the 1620s, when such wealthy men as Sir Christopher Hatton possessed princely estates comparable to those of "King" Carter in Virginia later. Blame for failure and delay was placed upon the character of the emigrants.

Ireland for these many years hath been the receptacle for our English runagates, that for their misled lives in England, do come running over to Ireland. Some for murder, some for theft; some that have spent themselves in riot and excess are driven over for debt, some come running over with other men's goods, some with other men's wives, but a great number now lately, that are more hurtful than all the rest, and those be recusants.

Thus wrote Barnaby Rich in *The Irish Hubbub* (1617).

Precisely as in a later century the name Canada or Australia was likely automatically to evoke the image of a remittance man, a ne'er-do-well, a runaway, or a criminal, so the Irish experience predetermined the image of the character of emigrants. Maryland, because of the Baltimores, is especially illuminating in this context. Thus in 1655, in "Virginia and Maryland, or The Lord Baltamore's printed Case, uncased and answered," it was hotly charged that the proprietor "now admits all sorts of Religions, and intended even 2000 Irish, and by his own Letters clears and indemnifies one, that said, Those Irish would not leave a Bible in Maryland." Of the Newport-Gates-Somers "supply" sent to Virginia even earlier, William Stith wrote in his *History of Virginia* that "a great Part of this new Company consisted of unruly Sparks, packed off by their Friends, to escape worse Destinies at home. And the rest were chiefly made up of poor Gentlemen, broken Tradesmen, Rakes and Libertines, Footmen, and such others, as were much fitter to spoil or ruin a Commonwealth, than to help to raise or maintain one." This

. . . seditious and distracted Rabble hath laid one of the finest Countries in *British America,* under the unjust Scandal of being a mere Hell upon Earth, another *Siberia,* and only fit for the Reception of Malefactors, and the vilest of the People. So that few People, at least few large Bodies of People have been induced, willingly to transport themselves to such a Place.

The custom of transporting felons to Virginia began, he thinks, with King James. Stith's acrid paragraphs go back to John Hammond's *Leah and Rachel* (1656) and earlier records, Hammond writing, for example, as we have seen: "Then were Jayls emptied, youth seduced, infamous women drilled in, the provisions all brought out of England, and that embezzlled by the Trustees." A minor but illuminating incident in this part of the world in 1648 I have already cited . . . In this episode on the Delaware Bay and River the Dutch replaced the English, but the compound of sordor, treachery, and cruelty is again woven into a single whole, the origins of which are, in large measure, from Tudor Ireland.

IV

But it is time to turn to the positive side of the picture and to examine the promotion literature in English of the early colonial period. It must not be forgotten that, whatever the power of the printed or written word among the upper and middle classes, the majority of Englishmen could not read—a fact that calls for severe scrutiny of certain hasty inferences sometimes drawn from this propaganda. Obviously the obligation laid upon this literature was to destroy the unfavorable image of colonizing and substitute a more alluring one. The literature was in this successful, inasmuch as colonies were founded, were nourished, and grew, and it has also had the unintended success of coloring all American origins with glamour.

Promotion literature falls into several distinguishable categories. The most impressive is the formal treatise on colonization, of which there are two sorts: treatises which, anticipating settlement, theorized, from inference or from the example of others, about the character of the potential colony; and treatises which drew felicitous inferences from English experience, once it had begun. The first type is mostly a sixteenth-century product, as in Hakluyt's *Discourse of Western Planting* (1584); the most illustrious example of the later type is probably Bacon's essay *Of Plantations* (1625). Secondly, one may associate with this type the general preferences or other introductory matter in collections of voyages or reports on colonial enterprises. The various volumes of the second edition of Hakluyt's *Principal Navigations* (1598-1600) have such prefaces, and the introductory pages to William Vaughan's ("Orpheus Iunior") *The Golden Fleece* (1626) and John Hammond's *Leah and Rachel* (1656) are of this sort. A third type is the official request to government for a patent, or the request plus the patent, published to persuade "adventurers" to invest and settlers to migrate; examples can be found in Brown's *Genesis of the United States,* and the "Instructions to the Colonists by Lord Baltimore" (1633) are of this order. A fourth type, often quoted in this study, is the reports of exploratory voyages. These commonly stress the economic plenitude of the new settlement, the healthiness of its situatïon, and the gentleness of the natives. Thomas Hariot's *A Briefe and true report of the new found land of Virginia* (1588) may be put in this category. In the fifth place the circulation of material having both official sanction and a personal tang is part of the picture, as in the "Coppie of a letter from Virginia . . . to the Councell of Virginia here in England," and such pamphlets as Robert Johnson's *Nova Britannia* and *A Trve Declaration of the estate of the Colonie in Virginia* (1610), a "confutation of such scandalous reports as haue tended to the disgrace of so worthy an enterprise." This was published "by aduise and direction of the Councell of Virginia." A sixth type, emanating from official authority, includes publication of the official laws and of regulations concerning the acquirement of land, both intended to assure the settler of the morality and good order of the enterprise, such as William Strachey's *Lavves Diuine, Morall and Martiall* of "Virginea Britannia" (1612). Seventh is that cleverest form of company-inspired propaganda, the official sermon on such an occasion as the departure of an important person for the colony, which appealed to the middle class and corrected wild talk in the taverns; an instance is Robert Gray's *A Good Speed to Virginia* (1609), dedicated to the Virginia Company. Finally, there is the personal report by an interested observer, such as Edward Winslow's *Good News From New England* (1624).

What are the chief themes of this promotion literature? One I have already touched upon in connection with Mediterranean colonial enterprise—the appeal to glory and heroism; and in English promotion literature, in apparent contradiction to what I have earlier remarked about the lack of influence of the Roman or Greek colony upon English theory, the sanction of antique heroism is frequently invoked. Thus Robert Johnson concluded his *Nova Britannia* (1609) by saying: "It would be my griefe and sorrow, to be exempted from the company of so many honourable minded men, and from this enterprise, tending to so many good endes, and then which, I truly thinke this day, there is not a worke of more excellent hope vnder the Sun, and farre excelling (all circumstances wayed) those Noble deedes of *Alexander, Hercules,* and those heathen Monarks, for which they were deemed Gods among their posterity." John White appealed to Roman example:

It is reported that when *Annibal* lay before *Rome,* it discouraged him much in his hopes of taking the Citty, that at the same instant there marched out of the Citty at contrary gates under their colours an Armie of souldiers towards the sea, to be shipped & sent over for a supply into *Spaine;* for it argued the *Romans* feared him not. . . .

Let the English therefore send out colonies. Crashaw appealed to Romulus and Remus as instances of the difficulty of founding a new nation; and William Strachey, in his *Historie of Travaile into Virginia Britannia* (it is true the work was not published until 1849), called upon the English to meditate upon antique virtue:

It is read that Themistocles hearing of the great victory that Melciades [Miltiades] had obtayned on the playne of Marathon, said, that that report would not lett him take any rest; and Julius Caesar wept at the sight of Alexander's image (who had at the yeares of twenty-four obtayned the name of Great), and cryed out: "Am I not miserable, that have done nothinge worthy of memory, and yet this prince at these yeares hath executed so many notable thinges?" Shall these, for the smoake of momentary glory, breake out thus passionate and forward? and shall not we, for the glory of our God be as affectionate [i.e., eager] and ambitious?

But these Renaissance flourishes conceivably were less compelling than appeals to Christian virtue. Sir Robert Gordon prophesied that all Christian after-ages would "eternize" the "shining brightnesse" of such men as Drake, Ralegh, Amadas, White, and others. Robert Gray in his sermon proclaimed that "the name, memorie and actions of those men doe only liue in the records of eternitie, which haue emploied their best endeuours in such vertuous and honourable enterprises, as haue aduanced the glorie of God, and inlarged the glorie and wealth of their countrie," and that therefore the fame of the Virginia Company would last as long as the sun and the moon. Nor was Captain John Smith unpersuaded of the value of a Christian sanction:

If he haue but the taste of virtue and magnanimitie, what to such a minde can bee more pleasant, then planting and building a foundation for his Posteritie, gotte from the rude earth, by Gods blessing and his owne industrie, without preiudice to any? If hee haue any graine of faith or zeale in Religion, what can hee doe less hurtfull to any: or more agreeable to God, then to seeke to conuert those poore Saluages to know Christ, and humanitie, whose labors with discretion will triple requite thy charge and paines?

"Our forefathers," wrote Robert Johnson, "not looking out in time, lost the prime and fairest proffer of the greatest wealth in the world, and wee taxe their omission for it, yet now it falles out, that wee their children are tryed in the like, there being yet an excellent portion left and by Diuine prouidence offered to our choice." Thus Protestant divinity paralleled the appeal of the Spanish crown, the Roman Catholic Church, and Las Casas.

The imperialism of the English, the Dutch, the Danes, and the Swedes, and the renewed energy of the French in the seventeenth century ran up against the established empires of Portugal and Spain, and in the case of England added religious rivalry to the rivalry for space. A second leading theme in the literature is, therefore, expansionism and the English right to empire. The examples of the Spanish and the Portuguese empires, wrote Peckham, should "minister just cause of incouragement to our Countreymen, not to account it so hard and difficult a thing for the subjects of this noble realme of England, to discover, people, plant and possesse the like goodly lands, and rich countreys not farre from us . . . not a little animate and encourage us to looke out and adventure abroad, understanding what large Countreys and Islands the Portugals with their small number have within these few yeeres discovered, peopled and planted." His doctrine echoed through scores of tracts, pamphlets, sermons, and the like vehicles of propaganda. Every part of the New World had its eager advocates, the idea being to "gaulle yhe King of Spain as yt wolde dyuerte hys forces, yhat hee troublethe these partes of Chrystendome wyth," and the persistent search for a Northwest Passage, like the persistent search for strategical colonies in the New World, was part of expansionist psychology arising in no small measure from fear and hatred of Spain. This theme gave Hakluyt one of his most splendid passages:

> . . . it can not be denied, but as in all former ages, [Englishmen] have bene men full of activity, stirrers abroad, and searchers of the remote parts of the world, so in this most famous and peerlesse government of her most excellent Majesty, her subjects through the speciall assistance, and blessing of God, in searching the most opposite corners and quarters of the world, and to speake plainly, in compassing the vaste globe of the earth more then once, have excelled all the nations and people of the earth. For, which of the kings of this land before her Majesty, had theyr banners ever seene in the Caspian sea? which of them hath ever dealt with the Emperor of Persia, as her Majesty hath done, and obteined for her merchants large & loving privileges? who ever saw before this regiment, an English Ligier in the stately porch of the Grand Signor at Constantinople? who ever found English Consuls & Agents at Tripolis in Syria, at Aleppo, at Babylon, at Balsara, and which is more, who ever heard of Englishman at Goa before now? what English shippes did heeretofore ever anker in the mighty river of Plate? passe and repasse the unpassable (in former opinion) straight of Magellan, range along the coast of Chili, Peru, and all the backside of Nova Hispania, further then any Christian ever passed, travers the mighty bredth of the South sea, land upon the Luzones in despight of the enemy, enter into alliance, amity, and traffike with the princes of the Moluccaes, & the Isle of Java, double the famous Cape of Bona Speranza, arive at the Isle of Santa Helena, & last of al returne home most richly laden with the commodities of China, as the subjects of this now flourishing monarchy have done?

This, to be sure, is the Elizabethan age speaking out loud and bold, but the carry-over into the Stuart monarchy was dynamic, so much so that the valuation put on colonies even as late as the time of Charles II placed English plantations in the West Indies ahead of the mainland colonies because they were better bases for intercepting Spanish trade. It must not be forgotten that to intercept the Spanish treasure fleet was somehow to create economic wealth in one's own country; European thinking about trade was strictly mercantilistic.

V

The attempt to rival the heroes of Plutarch, the call to convert the heathen, and the desire to expand the bounds of empire were, in the main, Renaissance values common to all the colonizing powers. We come closer to the English situation *per se* when we analyze the problem of population, the special appeal for trade, and the peculiar moral sanction on the English expressed in the promotion literature. That England was actually suffering from a glut of population at the end of the six-teenth century may be doubted, but that scores of writers thought the country was overcrowded is clear enough—alarm over social dislocation is one of the commonest notes in Tudor literature. The sixteenth century, as somebody has said, lived in terror of the tramp; and the sociological appeal of colonial promotion literature was alike to those fearful of anarchy, the socially dispossessed, and those fearful of being uprooted by the enclosure movement, the sale of the monastery lands, or the shifts in population by reason of the wool trade or some other rising industry. No appeal is more constant in the literature. Thus Gilbert, among the eight numbered reasons of "commodities" that "would ensue," once he found the Northwest Passage, declares: "Also we might inhabite some part of those countryes, and settle there such needy people of our countrey, which now trouble the common wealth, and through want here at home are inforced to commit outragious offences, whereby they are dayly consumed with the gallowes." In his *Divers Voyages* Richard Hakluyt lamented that the prisons were "pestered and filled with able men to serue their Countrie, which for small roberies are dayly hanged vp in great numbers" ("twentie at a clappe" in Rochester), who ought to be sent to the colonies and there usefully employed. In his *Discourse of Western Planting* he lamented that idle soldiers go "up and downe in swarms for lack of honest intertainment" and could be used against "stubborne Savages" who "shal refuse obedience to her Majestie." "Look seriously into the land," preached William Symonds, "and see whether there be not just cause, if not a necessity, to seek abroad. The people, blessed be God, do swarm in the land." And the great John Donne thought that colonization "shall redeeme many a wretch from the Lawes of death, from the hands of the Executioner, upon whom perchance a small fault, or perchance a first fault, or perchance a fault heartily and sincerely repented, perchance no fault, but malice, had otherwise cast a present and ignominious death." Patrick Copland that same year (1622) praised the officers of the city of London, "who seeing this Cittie to be mightily increased, and fearing lest the ouerflowing multitude of inhabit-ants should, like too much bloud in the body, infect the whole Cittie with *plague* and *pouertie*," urged "the transporting of their ouer-flowing multi-tude into *Virginia*."

Plantations were not merely to relieve the surplus population, they were to reform criminals, albeit there were those who asked for criminals in order that a particular colony might be held, and inconsistently com-plained of the kind of colonist they got. Thus Hammond, in his *Leah and Rachel*, though he paints a vivid picture of lawlessness at the begin-ning of his account, finds the Virginians undergoing a sea change into something new and strange, having become "generally affable, courteous and very assistant to strangers," theft "seldom or never committed . . . and although Doores are nightly left open (especially in the Summer time), Hedges hanging full of Cloathes, Plate frequently used amongst all comers and goers (and there is good store of Plate in many houses) yet I never heard of any losse."

The myth that the American Adam came to the New World and lost his innocence should, in some sense, be reversed; he came here to regain virtue. Francis Higginson wrote with pleasure that in New England children of five can set out corn, and exclaimed:

> Oh what a good worke might you that are rich do for your poore brethren, to helpe them with your purses onely to convey them hither with their children and familics, where they may live as well both for soule and body as any where in the world. . . . For when you are once parted with England you shall meete neither with taverns nor alehouse, nor butchers, nor grosers, nor apothecaries shops to helpe what things you need, in the midst of the great ocean, nor when you are come to land, here are yet neither markets nor fayres to buy what you want.

A letter from the Virginia Company to the City of London in 1609 expresses the wish to "ease the city and suburbs" of the idle:

> And if the inmate . . . shall demaund what may be theire present mayntenance, what maye be theire future hopes? it may please you to let them Knowe that for the present they shall have meate, drinke and clothing, with an howse, orchard and garden, for the meanest family, and a possession of lands to them and their posterity, one hundred acres for every man's person that hath a trade, or a body able to endure day labour, as much for his wief, as much for his child, that are of yeres to do service to the Colony, with further particular reward according to theire particular meritts and industry.

Forty years later in *A Perfect Description of Virginia* we read that "All kinds of Trades-men may live well there, and do gaine much by their labours and arts," that youths of sixteen and upward are wanted for apprentices and servants, "then to have Land given them, and Cattel to set them up," and that there is room for "thousands of these kinds of young boyes and maydens." The legend of the cleansing West begins, it is clear, not at the Mississippi but in London.

The results were inevitably contradictory. On the one hand the mainland colonies had to be pictured as a vast improvement over England, as Hammond does in *Leah and Rachel*:

> The Country is very full of sober, modest persons, both men and women, and many that truly fear God and follow that perfect rule of our blessed Saviour, to do as they would be done by; and of such happy inclination is the Country, that many who in England have been lewd and idle, there in

emulation or imitation (for example moves more than precept) of the industry of those they finde there, not onely grow ashamed of their former courses, but abhor to heare of them and in small time wipe off those stains they have formerly been tainted with.

On the other hand the literature is filled with complaints about the unruliness, lack of discipline, insubordination, and want of common sense exhibited by the common man during not only the period of exploration but also that of first settlement. We have already had some glimpse into the mutinous spirit of early Jamestown. Sir Ferdinando Gorges complained of the "idle proceedinges" of his colony on the New England coast, which "have mutch prejudcialld the publique good, deviding themselves into factions, each disgracing the other." English fishermen on the Maine coast were "worse than the very Savages, impudently and openly lying with their Women, teaching their Men to drinke drunke, to sweare and blaspheme the name of GOD, and in their drunken humour to fall together by the eares." And Edward Winslow complained of Weston's colony that among the causes of the "overthrow and bane" of plantations, the irresponsibility of those who send out men "endued with bestial, yea, diabolical affections" was important. It was all very puzzling. The writer of promotion literature was inevitably caught between liberty and authority—between the need of creating a small, quasi-feudal military garrison and trading post to keep order, and the appeal of laissez-faire principles, by which, abandoning any sort of communal responsibility, the settler could make his private fortune. Inevitably, however, the psychology of real-estate promotion won out; typical is R. Rich's *Nevves from Virginia:*

> To such as to Virginia
>   Do purpose to repaire;
> And when that they shall hither come,
>   Each man shall have his share,
>
> Day wages for the laborer,
>   And for his more content,
> A house and garden plot shall have,
>   Besides 'tis further ment
>
> That every man shall have a part,
>   And not thereof denied
> Of generall profit, as if that he
>   Twelve pounds, ten shillings paid.

The concept of communal enterprise gave way to obstreperous individualism.

But was it lawful to intrude upon the savages? Was it right to claim sovereignty over lands that conceivably belonged to the Emperor of China, or, if not to him, then to the Emperor Powhatan? The Spanish and the Portuguese had had their ethical problem solved for them by the pope; the Protestant English not only had no pope but desired to oust the Spaniards from as much of the New World as they could, at the same time assuring settlers it was lawful for them to colonize. They appealed therefore to the law of nature and to the Bible, intermingling the two appeals. And inasmuch as the English were obviously the successors of the Chosen People as the Spanish were not, the argument, especially as against the Indians, was comforting.

"Their land," wrote Robert Cushman, "is spacious and void," the Indians "do but run over the grass, as do also the foxes and wild beasts"; wherefore, "as the ancient Patriarchs therefore removed from straiter places unto more roomthy . . . so it is lawful now to take a land, which none useth; and make use of it." God, argued John Winthrop, gave the earth to man—"why then should we stand starving here for places of habitation?" John White held the same opinion:

> If it were then the minde of God, that man should possesse all parts of the earth, it must be enforced that we neglect our duty, and crosse his will, if we doe it not, when wee have occasion and opportunitie. . . . It cannot be denied but the life of man is every way made more comfortable, and afforded a more plentiful supply in a larger scope of ground, which moves men to bee so insatiable in their desires to joyne house to house, and land to land, till there be no more place . . . the husbanding of unmanured grounds, and shifting into empty Lands, enforceth men to frugalitie, and quickneth invention: and the setling of new States requireth justice and affection to the common good: and the taking of large Countreys presents a naturall remedy against couetousnesse, fraud, and violence.

Even Thomas Morton of Merry Mount fame ironically reproduced the argument—God had swept away "heapes" of savages "for the propagation of the Church of Christ."

For a new Canaan had been appointed for English Protestants, and to the Elizabethan or Jacobean Englishman there was no disharmony between the argument for individual gain and the argument of religious glory. In 1578 Anthony Parkhurst wrote Hakluyt that God would prosper His faithful if they would but obey His commands:

> Such is the malice of wicked men the devils instruments in this our age, that they cannot suffer any thing . . . to proceed and prosper that tendeth to the setting forth of Gods glory, and the amplifying of the Christian faith, wherein hitherto princes have not bene so diligent as their calling required. . . . I trust God hath made you an instrument to increase the number, and to moove

men of power, to redeeme the people of Newfoundland and those parts from out of the captivitie of that spirituall Pharao, the devil.

If the Indians could not be converted "Apostolically, without the helpe of man" nor "merely imperiallie, when a Prince, hath conquered their bodies, that the Preachers may feede their soules," but only "by way of marchandizing and trade," then let the English "buy the pearles of earth" and sell "the pearles of heauen." Why not? Adam and Noah, said the Reverend John Cotton, were told to multiply and replenish the earth, and God directs the migrations of people which follow. "This may teach us all where we doe now dwell, or where after we may dwell, be sure you looke at every place appointed to you, from the hand of God: wee may not rush into any place, and never say to God, By your leave; but wee must discerne how God appoints us this place." There was, however, no doubt that God appointed Massachusetts Bay for His holy colony.

Scores of tracts enforced similar arguments. In his sermon of 1609 the Reverend William Crashaw had waxed eloquent in italics:

The Israelites had a *commandement* from God to dwell in *Canaan,* we haue *leaue* to dwell in *Virginea:* they were *commanded to kill* the heathen, we are *forbidden to kill them,* but are commanded to *conuert* them: they were *mighty* people, ours are *ordinarie:* they *armed,* ours *naked:* they had *walled townes,* ours haue scarce *houels* to couer them: that land flowed with *milke and honie,* our[s] abounds with as *good or better:* they sent men to search *that,* so we to search *this:* they brought of the *commodities,* so haue we: many *slandered* that countrey, so they doe of ours: more *beleeued* the slander then the trueth, and so they doe in ours: yet some stoode boldly for the *trueth,* and so there doe in ours, and better then those that doe depraue it.

If English beginnings were poor and small, Crashaw pointed out that the Israelites went down into Egypt but seventy souls and increased to six hundred thousand. And the stately John Winthrop not only agreed that Christians have warrant to occupy waste lands, following Biblical precedent, but appealed to the law of nature: "That which is common to all is proper to none. This savage people ruleth over many lands without title or property; for they inclose no ground, neither have they cattell to maintayne it, but remove their dwellings as they have occasion."

Doubtless these arguments were inconsistent. How appeal to the law of nature, which gives the earth to all men, and simultaneously insist that therefore you have the right to bring any portion of the earth that is "waste" under your dominion? How reconcile the appeal of a laissez-faire existence beyond the wildest dreams of the Jacobean world with the argument that "the setling of new States requireth justice and affection to the common good"? Why if the appeal to antique virtue was proper to the English at the end of the sixteenth century, was "the Portingales time

. . . out of date"? How reconcile praise of the "constant resolutions" and "incomparable honour" of the Iberians with casting them in the role of "Midianites" to be overcome by that stout Gideon's band, the English? The Elizabethans and the Jacobeans, like us, found no difficulty in entertaining two or more contradictory notions at one and the same time; they resolved these inconsistencies as John White resolved them toward the conclusion of his *The Planters Plea:*

If in the Worlds infancy, men out of an ambitious humour, or at present for private advantages and expectation of gaine, thrust themselves out from their owne dwellings into parts farre remote from their native soyle; why should not we conceive, that if they doe this for a corruptible crowne; that the desire and expectations of an incorruptible . . . may as strongly allure such as by patient continuance in well-doing seeke immortalitie & life?

The complex origins of the colonial idea in England, the immense and contradictory elements that contributed to its growth and that led to the planting of mainland colonies of Englishmen in the New World show not only that the pristine image of a new Eden had already been criss-crossed with darker shades of doubt and selfishness, but require us also to be cautious in adopting simplicistic notions that an American dream somehow mysteriously broke down in the nineteenth or twentieth century. Insofar as the origins of the American idea go back to the planting of the first mainland colonies by the English, these origins are as conflicting, inconsistent, and difficult to identify as the components of other great episodes in the history of Western man. "America" did not descend directly from Eden.

The French Empire in Canada:
Image of the Old World

KENNETH D. McRAE

The history of the French in Canada has become even more stereotyped than the Pilgrim-Pocahontas-William Penn story which Howard Mumford Jones dispels. It is generally seen as a narrative of indefatigable Jesuits plying the rivers and lakes of the primitive north country, attempting to win converts to their one true faith, and of rough-hewn fur traders—independent, tough, resourceful—as Indian in their way as the savages with whom they traded. In this selection, however, Professor Kenneth D. McRae of Carleton University goes beyond the activities of the Jesuits and the *coureurs de bois* to analyze the French imperial structure. Accepting without comment the French mystique in the search for "gold" and "souls," he concentrates upon the effort to mold colonial "subjects" and imperial relationships in the image of the France of Louis XIV.

McRae's treatment invites comparison with the conclusions of Wolf and Jones. If, in effect, the Spanish crown and the early conquerors, priests, and officials sought to create a new utopia overseas, why could not France, with a remarkably unitary state already in existence at the time of its colonial endeavor, achieve greater success? Did the open frontier in both English and French America doom all dreams of establishing a permanently cohesive empire? In contrast to the English, why did the French limit rather than encourage the emigration of undesirables? Can one see in the ideologies of empire this early in the development of the New World forebodings of the loss of New France to foreign enemies and of British and Spanish America to rebellion and separation?

Above all, McRae highlights the problem with which we began. At their roots the drives for empire appear remarkably similar: Each was shaped by historical accident, by domestic developments, and by the New World environment. But there were, despite the similarities, subtle differences as well. The

From "The Structure of Canadian History," by Kenneth D. McRae in *The Founding of New Societies,* © 1964, by Louis Hartz. Reprinted by permission of Harcourt, Brace & World, Inc.

principal task of the comparative historian is to understand and explain not only why these similarities and differences occurred but also how they affected colonial development.

CONCERNING THE FRENCH COLONIAL EXPERIENCE, THE QUESTION OF timing is crucial. The significant date is not 1535, when Cartier explored the St. Lawrence to Montreal and wintered in Quebec, nor is it 1608, when Champlain established the first permanent settlement, but rather 1663, the year in which a struggling and still-insignificant colony was transferred from the Company of New France to direct royal control. For the earliest developments are in some respects at variance with the later character of the colony. Under a succession of chartered trading companies, colonization and settlement had been thoroughly subordinated to the fur trade, despite undertakings to the contrary. Several of the earliest concessionaires had been Huguenots, a far cry from the religious uniformity of later years. There was, then, an initial fleeting, commercial, bourgeois—even semiliberal—phase to the French experience in Canada, but this tendency was soon superseded. In the long run New France bore the imprint not of the age of Henri IV,[1] but of the age of Louis XIV and his great minister Colbert.

By the sixteen-sixties the doctrines and practice of absolutism in France had reached their highest peak. The Fronde,[2] that last, futile assertion of feudal particularism by a politically decadent nobility, had been suppressed. The King himself took full control of all aspects of government. His position was acknowledged with adulation by a society imbued with absolutist principles. The veneration for royal authority shown by Bossuet, the great apologist of divine right, is hardly less evident in the Huguenot[3] divines, whose coreligionists were to suffer so drastically when that authority was turned in full force against them. Like the Tudor monarchs of a century earlier, the French monarch had the solid backing of the bulk of the bourgeoisie, and the royal bureaucracy was drawn chiefly from their ranks. Absolutism was a progressive force, a unifying force, a successful and powerful instrument of a dynamic state. Its universal popularity lay in the fact that, to all appearances, it had made France by far the greatest nation in the world.

The effects of absolutism were felt in every branch of public policy. In

---

[1] ED. NOTE: Henry of Navarre, King of France (1589-1610).

[2] ED. NOTE: A revolt of the French nobility, 1648-1653, during the youth of Louis XIV.

[3] ED. NOTE: French Calvinists.

the economic sphere a vigorous mercantilist policy was the counterpart to political centralization. The army was reorganized and reshaped into a highly efficient instrument of state policy. Religious orthodoxy was made complete by the total revocation in 1685 of the Edict of Nantes.[4] In the light of the disasters that plagued the final decades of Louis XIV's long reign, his political system may appear more a façade than a reality, but this perspective is inappropriate here. In Canada the first and most active phase of royal government, the phase that stamped the character of the colony, occurred in the years immediately following 1663, when the star of absolutism was unmistakably in the ascendant.

It is necessary to pause briefly to insist on the significance of this point. New France was a projection—a deliberate and official projection —into the New World of a dynamic, authoritarian society at the zenith of its power. This does not mean that the colony became an ideal model, or even a mirror image, of the mother country; the rough conditions of a colonial society prevented that. But it does mean that in its law and institutions the colony reflected the prevailing ethos of authoritarianism to an even greater degree than did the more complex and less malleable society of old France. If it is basically true, as has been argued of the English colonies, that "America was settled by men who fled from the feudal and clerical oppressions of the Old World," such a generalization cannot hold true for French Canada. In this fact lies the first and most fundamental difference between the English and the French traditions in North America. The early English colonies were liberal, heterodox offshoots of a society already deeply divided within itself. French Canada was the closely controlled projection of a highly centralized regime. Though both societies might believe in principle that colonies should exist for the benefit of the mother country, though both might be mercantilist in economic policy, there was yet room for considerable divergence as to the latitude to be permitted to the colonists.

If the English colonies were by the very circumstances of their foundation born free, that is, born with a prevailing ethos of religious dissent, individual freedom, and limited government, it is equally clear that freedom in New France—and it existed incontestably in substantial measure —was a matter not of doctrine, but of circumstance and accident. First and foremost, it arose from the geographical environment, from the long and uncertain delay in communication with France, from the physical inability of officials to control the vast geographic empire that was French America. Second, it arose from conflicts within the institutional structure, from the differing and occasionally clashing interests of church

---

[4] ED. NOTE: The Edict of Nantes, 1598, gave the Huguenots certain political and religious privileges and a measure of tolerance.

and state, from rivalry between governor and intendant. Finally, it arose from neglect. The magnitude of France's involvement in Europe relegated colonial affairs to insignificance for long periods.

It is this theme of theoretical absolutism—albeit a paternalistic and well-meaning absolutism—tempered by practical difficulties in its application that provides the most comprehensible conceptual framework for the study of New France. In the political and administrative sphere it can be documented in the roles of the governor, the intendant, and the Sovereign Council. In a military sense absolutism brought badly needed security, for the arrival of royal troops in 1665 rescued the infant colony from the menace of extinction at the hands of the Iroquois. In economic policy the doctrine can be seen in the regulation of prices, in the sponsoring of secondary industries, and in control of the fur trade, the colony's only staple export. Economic control was facilitated by geography; there was no seacoast fit for smuggling, and the monopolistic nature of the St. Lawrence route meant easy control of imports. In the fur trade, however, regulation could not be pushed too far, owing to competition of traders from Hudson Bay and from the English colonies to the south. In the religious sphere, the early missionary work of the Jesuits and the tireless organizing talents of François de Laval, first Bishop of Quebec, rapidly laid the foundations for a strong ecclesiastical authority. After 1627 few Huguenots reached New France, and the handful who did were carefully watched. The occasional trader might visit the colony briefly, but Protestants were forbidden to winter there unless engaged in the king's service. At the end of the French regime, Masères could record the presence of only three Protestant families.

The most striking illustration of the theme of absolutism is the seigneurial system of land tenure. An edict of 1664 established the Custom of Paris as the legal system of the colony, and in the land law this meant that New France possessed what would appear at first glance to be an exact replica of the feudalism of Europe, a feudalism already in decline. Lands were granted en seigneurie, as indeed had been the case since the earliest grants during the sixteen-twenties. Seigneurs swore fealty and homage to the Crown on taking possession of their seigneuries. Minerals were reserved to the Crown, as were oak trees for shipbuilding. Seigneuries transferred otherwise than by direct descent were subject to the droit de quint, a tax of one-fifth of their value.

Similarly, the habitant owed a series of feudal obligations to the seigneur. There were the cens et rentes, paid annually, and the lods et ventes, an irregular mutation fine corresponding to the seigneur's quint. There were the banalités, of which the droit de mouture, or seigneur's milling right, was the principal one exercised in Canada. The droit de *four banal,* or right of oven banality, was rarely attempted in Canada. The *corvée* required the habitant to work several days each year for the seigneur, the exact number being fixed by custom. Other minor rights, such as the reservation of wood, sand, and stone, or the levy on fish, or the right of ferry, are worth a passing mention if only to complete the picture. Many of the seigneurs were granted judicial rights, often with full powers of *haute, moyenne, et basse justice,* but high jurisdiction was infrequently exercised, and in any case appeals were always open to the royal courts.

Yet closer examination will show that when feudal tenure was transplanted its spirit was necessarily transformed. Certain of the seigneurial payments, such as the *cens et rentes,* were little more than nominal, and others were seldom enforced. The *corvée* seems to have been imposed lightly, seldom more than six days per year, often only three. In a small pioneer settlement the seigneur frequently found that the milling banality was more of a financial burden than a boon, but it was his obligation no less than his right. Justice, administered informally by the seigneur in person, was certainly never the source of revenue that it was in France.

On behalf of the habitants the royal administration intervened vigorously to check attempted abuses and extortion by the seigneurs, as well as to enforce fulfillment of their obligations. Far from being an unchecked source of oppression for an overburdened peasantry, as they were in France, the seigneurs in Canada became in effect the unsalaried agents of the Crown for the settlement of the colony. In France feudalism merely supported a privileged order that had lost its social function; in New France seigneurialism, not unlike the European feudalism of an earlier age, regained some of its primitive rationale in providing elements of security, order, and social cohesion in an environment ringed about with potential dangers. It is possible to regard Canadian feudalism as a mere anachronism, accidentally carried to the New World. Some aspects of it undoubtedly were vestigial, but behind the façade there stands at least one towering reality: the continuing concern of the central authorities for regulating even the minor details of rural life.

The essence of Canadian feudalism is its mildness, its relaxation, its absence of systematic harshness or oppression. The proof of this lies in the almost incredible survival of seigneurial tenure long after the end of the French regime, despite increasing difficulties owing to population pressure and subdivision of holdings. Feudal dues and obligations were not terminated until 1854, and even at this date the rights of the seigneurs were merely converted into fixed annual rentals which the habitant could pay off in a lump sum capitalized at six per cent. But few chose this alternative; the majority continued to pay the annual rental.

Only in 1935 did the Quebec legislature incorporate a syndicate to borrow funds at low interest and buy out the remaining rights of the seigneurs. The farmers were then to repay principal and interest to the syndicate at a rate equal to the former annual rental. In this way it is now expected that these last vestiges of feudal tenure will disappear sometime in 1969 or 1970.

It was the very mildness of feudalism and indeed of the whole structure of absolutism that preserved the institutions of French Canada from revolutionary overthrow. The ultimate reason for this mildness lies in the conditions of the frontier. The structure of absolutism in French Canada was rather like a sieve: as soon as pressure was applied, there was an escape through the meshes to freedom outside the settlements. The tighter the web of control, the more appealing became the life of freedom in the forests. From the very beginning the *coureur de bois*[5] emerged as a distinct social type, embracing Indian ways and living off the fur trade, a continuing source of concern to both secular and ecclesiastical authorities. In this easy alternative to absolutism lies an important clue to the moderation of government policy in general, to the mildness of feudal obligations, to the light incidence of ecclesiastical tithes, to the chronic ineffectiveness of the system of economic controls. If an open, nonhostile frontier provides an escape valve in any new society, it becomes proportionately more troublesome and more debilitating to the extent that the colony is built upon authoritarian foundations.

The flow of immigration to the colony was disappointingly small. The one significant wave came during the early years of royal rule under the brief but all-important *intendance* of Jean Talon (1665-1672). The population increased from 3,215 at the census of 1665 to 6,705 in 1673, and to 9,677 in 1681. After this date immigration declined very sharply, and one severely limiting factor was an almost morbid reluctance of the French authorities to depopulate France in order to build up the colony. All in all, though only rough figures can be devised, it is estimated that total immigration to Canada during the entire French regime was at most 10,000 persons, and about one-quarter of these came during the brief Talon period. The immigrants were carefully selected in France and rigorously inspected on arrival in the colony, often by the intendant in person. Physical robustness, youth, unimpeachable religious orthodoxy, and—for the women at least—good moral character were the principal qualifications demanded.

Despite the strong element of government control and screening, the colonization of New France was overwhelmingly a voluntary one. Though large numbers achieved passage to the colony by means of a

[5] ED. NOTE: French fur trader and Indian agent.

system of indenture for three years, these obligations were undertaken willingly in the hope of personal betterment. For more than a century, the transportation of convicts was unknown in Canada. Only in 1723 did the home authorities, over strenuous protests from the colony, send a first small contingent of minor law-breakers, mainly smugglers and poachers, to strengthen the desperately small trickle of immigrants. Characteristically, even the convicts were carefully selected *"bons hommes"* drawn from the royal prisons. On arrival they were enrolled in the ordinary indenture system and quickly absorbed into the life of the colony. The experiment was relatively successful, and protests soon faded, but at this late date the small number of deportees left no visible impression on a society whose main outlines were already firmly established. What is significant is the prolonged hesitation in sending prisoners. The reason is one that can be illustrated time after time: in the framework of absolutism, the colony was to represent the quintessence of the virtues of the parent society; its vices were to be filtered out in the process of fragmentation.

Since immigration became negligible after the sixteen-eighties, later population growth depended very largely upon natural increase. In an environment already highly favorable, governmental policy imported young girls to balance the sexes, paid cash premiums for early marriages, fined bachelors and denied them trading rights, and provided liberal pensions for families of ten or more children. Under these stimuli New France achieved a fertility rate among the highest ever recorded, and with only modest assistance from immigration the population increased to 13,815 in 1698, to 24,434 in 1720 and to 42,701 in 1739, and 55,009 in 1754, the last census of the French regime.

But it was not enough. The original base of immigrants was too small. While New France was doggedly building her population to 55,000, the English colonies had grown to well over a million inhabitants during the same century and a half of settlement, even though the population of metropolitan France was probably twice that of Great Britain. One basic weakness of France is not difficult to identify. While only a few thousand carefully screened settlers were trickling to Canada, almost simultaneously some 200,000 Huguenot exiles were driven from their homeland after the revocation of the Edict of Nantes, to establish themselves in Germany, Holland, England, South Africa, and even the rival English colonies in America. The effects on France itself were severe enough, but for Canada the consequences were even more profound. Had the colony offered a place of refuge, an escape for dissenters on New England lines, for even a modest fraction of these exiles, the subsequent history of North America might have been vastly different.

It is not easy to portray in a few lines the social structure of the colony, and one should avoid the pitfall of trying to extrapolate backwards from the truncated society that existed under the first decades of British rule. In the rural areas, there was no wide social or economic gap between habitant and seigneur, nor could there be under frontier conditions. Quite a few seigneurs were of modest origins, merchants, officials, or even habitants. Those who tried to live like independent gentlemen soon sank into penury and literal starvation. Only a small number of seigneurs belonged to the nobility, and practically all of these were colonials ennobled in Canada. Even this group did not constitute a legally privileged order. Unlike their counterparts in France, they were free to engage in trade. They had no exemptions from export or import duties (or from the *taille*,[6] since the latter was never levied in Canada), they paid tithes, and they were equal to the habitants before the law.

If New World conditions leveled down the seigneur, they clearly raised the habitant to a condition well above that of the French peasant. Though life was hard and luxury non-existent, there is abundant testimony from European visitors as to the rude sufficiency and even comfort of his life, his fine physique, politeness, dignity, cheerfulness, and attachment to religion. Not all of the testimony is favorable. There are references to vanity, laziness, wastefulness, stubbornness, improvidence. But these merely prove the point, for these are the vices of the man who feels himself well off.

The urban population is far more difficult to characterize, and it was not a negligible element. In the census of 1698 Quebec accounted for almost 2,000 and Montreal almost 1,200 of a total of 13,815. Together they represent much the same proportion in 1754, nearly 13,000 in a total of 55,009. As might be expected under a paternalistic regime, a large sector of this population was made up of civilian officials, garrison troops, and workers in government enterprises such as the naval shipyards at Quebec. Commerce was a significant element in the colony's economy, but it is difficult to discern any sizable independent bourgeoisie. Small merchants and retailers and a few wealthy fur traders were certainly in evidence, but even in the prosperous years of the eighteenth century the colony had only a handful of reasonably prosperous families, and these few tended to develop close links with officialdom. Much of the important export trade was carried on by employees of merchants resident in France, merchants whose connection with the colony remained tenuous. Similarly, although the professional classes were ably represented by a few outstanding individuals, their numbers were small. Even the Catholic clergy, profoundly influential in town and country

[6] ED. NOTE: A direct tax levied on personal property.

alike, were surprisingly few in relation to their vast spiritual and educational responsibilities. Thus although urban life was well established, the mentality of an independent middle class with its roots in the colony was not.

Perhaps the best way to comprehend the society of New France is to identify those elements in metropolitan society that were absent from the colony. First, there were no Huguenots, practically speaking. The unity of Catholic doctrine was unchallenged; even Jansenists[7] were all but unknown. Second, there were very few examples of the old French nobility. Third—and most striking—no *avocat*[8] was permitted to practice his profession in the colony, most legal matters being handled by notaries. Nor was there an independent, hereditary judiciary as in France, the principal court being the appointed Sovereign Council. It is no coincidence that the very groups which had held out the longest against the triumph of absolutism in the mother country found no place in the life of the colony. It is also significant that Canada possessed no printing press throughout the entire French regime.

In the eighteenth century there is a visible and widening gulf between French Canadians and Frenchmen from France, a consciousness of separate interests and separate identities. In other words, the traditionalism of the fragment is already asserting itself. The beginnings may be discerned around 1700. By this date immigration had fallen off sharply, and no doubt a considerable majority of the population were Canadian born. The following decades saw economic progress, material comfort, and a growing self-confidence. From the Treaty of Utrecht in 1713 to the War of the Austrian Succession in 1744, New France enjoyed an unprecedented peace, a brief respite which enabled the culture to consolidate itself. For many historians these three tranquil decades constitute the Golden Age of New France, and they could not have come more opportunely, in view of the ordeal that lay ahead.

The evidence of this hardening of identity is not difficult to find. In 1725 the Governor, Vaudreuil, commented that a "spirit of rebelliousness and independence" permeated the whole colony. The intendant Hocquart comes even closer to the mark: "They are," he writes of the Canadians in 1736, *"naturellement indociles."* This general intractability forced the modification or even abandonment of many an ill-considered official policy, yet it occurs in a society that remains technically absolutist.

[7] ED. NOTE: Followers of Cornelius Jansen, a seventeenth-century Dutch bishop, who, enamored of the ideas of Saint Augustine, preached the importance of faith over works as a means of obtaining God's grace.

[8] ED. NOTE: Lawyer.

There is a relationship here that deserves careful analysis. Legally speaking, the absolutist ethos continued, but the character of the colony checked its excesses and prevented it from slipping into despotism, thereby assuring for Canada an eighteenth century far different from the eighteenth century in France. For absolutism in Canada remained inescapably a moderate absolutism, a doctrine that could evoke no such stark antithesis between the real and the rational as inspired the Enlightenment in France. The main writings of the Enlightenment were not unknown in the colony, though their circulation was restricted by ecclesiastical censorship. But the crucial point was that they lacked explosive potentiality. Though the fuse might be available, there was no keg of powder to explode. The whole issue may be reduced to a simple series of propositions. Because legal absolutism found natural limits in the conditions of the new society, there could be no despotism. If no despotism, there could be no revolution. If no revolution, then the absolutist ethos was bound to persist, however subtly it might be transmuted, in some form or other, as in fact it does even to the present day.

COLONIAL SOCIETY

The Baroque Society
of Hispanic America

IRVING A. LEONARD

Although the imperial urges of England, France, and Spain were broadly similar, the European response to the colonial environment was remarkably different. In creating a colonial society each met the problem of a labor force in a different way; each sought to assure internal peace and order in its own fashion; each developed a social structure different from the other two. Yet despite their uniqueness, analysis of ways in which each approached colonial problems and created colonial institutions helps to illuminate the accomplishments and to highlight the peculiarities of the others.

Reprinted from *Baroque Times in Old Mexico* by Irving A. Leonard by permission of The University of Michigan Press. Ch. III, pp. 37-52. Copyright © 1959 by The University of Michigan.

The first essay in this section analyzes seventeenth-century Mexican society as a prototype for all Spanish America. Its author, Irving A. Leonard, for many years professor of Hispanic American history and literature at the University of Michigan, has spent his scholarly life studying Spanish colonial culture. He emphasizes here the baroque quality of Mexican society—"profusion of ethnological detail, intricate hierarchy, and superstitious credulity." The term "baroque," he feels, is particularly apt, suggesting as it does a parallel in the complexity, diffusion, and tension of that mode in art and architecture.

Spanish colonial society fits the metaphor well. The product of local conditions as much as of conscious planning, it was made up of a myriad of castes and classes. The Indian, despite decimation by pestilence and mistreatment (the central valley of Mexico lost over 90 percent of its Indian inhabitants within a century after the arrival of Cortés), became an integral part of Spanish colonial life. His intermarriage with the white and the Negro ultimately created an infinitely complex social structure, unparalleled in either English or French America. Reading Irving Leonard's description, one cannot escape the dominant theme of race with its divisive and stabilizing effects and its tremendous influence upon the structure of Spanish colonial society as a whole. How the existence of a large, sedentary Indian population would have affected the English or French in the New World is a vital question for the student of comparative history.

I T WAS THE INHABITANTS OF NEW SPAIN WHO OFFERED THE MOST vital expression of the Baroque complexity of their time and place. From the very beginning of Spanish rule a stratified society developed, the ethnic roots of which reached back to Asia through the Indians, to Africa through the Negroes, and to Europe through the Spaniards. The existence of these disparate elements side by side and the inevitable fusion resulting from association soon produced a strange ethnic conglomerate of almost kaleidoscopic diversity. Within this unequal partnership arose a complex system of tensions between men, colors, classes, and races that in

. . . all this inner unsteadiness, seething within a world kept in a thrice secular peace and security from European wars, everything contributed to make the soul of the Indies something strange and rare, almost unique in the annals of the human spirit.

If profusion of detail and hierarchy are among the typical characteristics of the Baroque, they were increasingly present in the ethnic composition of the neomedieval communities of the New World. As the seventeenth century advanced Hispanic civilization sank its roots so deeply in the Spanish American soil that its patterns are discernible three centuries later. Ever more intricate did the constellation of class and caste grow as a prolific miscegenation progressed. And the very fluidity of this ethnic process, which was creating entirely new human species, helped to insure the stability of a neomedieval order. The multiplicity of racial types emerging from a sort of Baroque melting pot gave a sociological expression of the political maxim "divide and rule" to which Spanish policy was securely wedded. By diligently fostering a kind of "pigmentocracy," with caste distinctions based largely on the amount of white blood in an individual's veins, the possibility was slight that sufficient cohesion might develop among the exploited masses to tempt them to challenge the control of the privileged white minority. But a closer scrutiny of the components of this Baroque society is in order.

The basic racial elements, as already indicated, were American, African, and European, together with resulting mixtures. Within each of these groups, however, social and psychological differences tended to compound mutual antagonisms, though prejudices stemmed much less from differences of pigment than in the English and French colonies. Blood played a part in determining position in the Spanish American hierarchy, but antipathies sprang more from the social discrimination maintained by rigid barriers which persons of color occasionally scaled. Though the Indian was the original and numerically the largest element of this New World cosmos, his lowly status in the social organism suggests a more inverted approach to the discussion by considering first the dominant white minority.

All too often the term "Spaniard" implies a collective identity, or a fairly precise national type. It is usually assumed that all individuals so designated have, in general, a common appearance, psychology, and language that give them a recognized national pattern. While such simplification is at all times hazardous, it is peculiarly unsafe when applied to the highly individualistic peoples of the Spanish Peninsula, particularly when nationalism itself was still in swaddling clothes. Shaped into more or less isolated compartments by its irregular topography and moulded by historical circumstances, Spain has long been characterized by a regionalism so pronounced as to endow its inhabitants with striking contrasts of temperament, appearance, and language. The gay Andalusian of the south, the sober Castilian of the central north, the laborious Gallician of the northwest, the enterprising Catalan of the east, the alien, industrious Basque of the northeast, are all "Spaniards" who present traits of character, psychology, and speech so diverse and so dissimilar as to form distinct peoples. This almost Baroque profusion of ethnic detail among the Peninsulars has played a part in retarding national unification in Spain down to the present time.

Owing to the celebrity of Cortés, Alvarado, Pizarro, and many other conquistadors, together with a certain similarity of the Spanish spoken in America to that in Andalucía, a belief was long current that the conquerors and early settlers came almost exclusively from southern Spain. This theory is no longer tenable, particularly when applied to the Baroque seventeenth century. While the men who accompanied Columbus on his first two voyages were probably all from Andalucía, as early as 1506 it was plainly evident that, politically at least, the Aragonese were dominant in Hispaniola, or Santo Domingo. Early chronicles and passenger lists indicate that about forty-two per cent of the emigration was from the southern region of the Peninsula. Nearly an equal percentage came from Castile; the balance originated in other parts of Spain bordering on these central provinces, including Portugal, the Balearic and Canary islands. This early preponderance of Castilians and Andalusians is explained by the monopoly exercised by Castile from the outset in the affairs of the Indies. It is unfortunate, perhaps, that this tended to restrict the migration of Basques, Galicians, and Catalans whose thrift and industry admirably equipped them for the task of developing economically the new colonies. But well before the seventeenth century these restrictions were so far relaxed that immigration in the New World represented a cross section of the peoples of Spain.

So strong were linguistic bonds and provincial affinities of these groups, however, that they tended to reproduce in the New World much of the regionalism of the mother country by congregating in certain localities and in *barrios* or districts of the larger towns and cities. In the new environments old world jealousies and antagonisms acquired renewed vitality, occasionally exploding into open feuds and violent clashes attended by loss of life. These enmities were visible even in the military phase of the Conquest. When the troubled Aztec monarch, Montezuma, held captive by Cortés, was informed that other Spaniards under Narváez had come to arrest his captor, he was doubtless puzzled by the explanation offered him.

. . . We came from Castile itself, which is called Old Castile, and we called ourselves Castilians, and the Captain (Narváez) who was now at Cempoala, and the people he had brought with him, came from another province, named Biscaya and they called themselves Biscayans, and spoke like the Otomís of this land of Mexico.

This last phrase clearly implied that the Basque language used by Narváez' followers was as outlandish as the Indian language mentioned was to Montezuma. These festering antipathies of Spanish regionalism brought much dissension and disunity among the dominant whites throughout the colonial era, including the religious communities in which the particularism of the old country was occasionally stronger than the vows of Christian brotherhood.

The frequent absence of cordiality among Spaniards of different provincial origin was only one of the discords afflicting the relations of the ruling classes. Even more widespread and vehement was the disaffection traceable to differing official status and social strata. The top administrative and judicial posts were uniformly reserved for Court favorites of the King in Madrid, and many of the lesser offices of a swollen colonial bureaucracy went to Peninsular-born individuals by appointment or, as the financial affairs of the Hapsburgs worsened, by purchase irrespective of merit. Each viceroy usually arrived with a populous retinue of servants, relatives, friends, and hangers-on for whom sinecures were procured or the acquisition of choice property was facilitated. The bait of a title, or the prestige accruing from the mere fact of being European-born, enabled many Spaniards in impecunious circumstances to contract marriages with daughters of wealthy families who willingly bestowed fabulous dowries. Not all new arrivals were so fortunate, and the failure to fulfill similar anticipations left them singularly incapable of admiring the luckier ones. But even more bitter was the resentment of the American-born descendants of the conquistadors and first settlers called Creoles. With envy and anger they saw the fruits of the blood, sweat, and swords of their ancestors consumed by haughty adventurers and newly powerful parvenus. The get-rich-quick philosophy of this parasitic upperclass inevitably poisoned the relations of the dominant whites, and the comparatively small minority of Europeans and American-born burned with passionate feelings of hostility and contempt.

The futile efforts of Hapsburg Spain to check the tide of heterodoxy in Europe by endless wars were destroying its solvency and depopulating its fields. The drain on manpower was not caused by the armies alone, but by the emigration of the more energetic of the humbler classes who, increasingly in the seventeenth century, poured into the Indies. These immigrant peasants and artisans frequently began life in the new environment as itinerant peddlers and small tradesmen. By dint of industry and frugal habits they often amassed a small fortune in a relatively short time. Though many were nearly illiterate and possessed none of the social graces, their thrift and stability, added to a European origin, gave them a certain luster in the eyes of the American-born Spanish women who found their own men much too fickle and irresponsible. Occasionally these *nouveaux riches* of male persuasion presumed on these favors and contracted unions which brought down upon them and their offspring the wrath of relatives with aristocratic pretensions but often of less pure white blood. Where marriages of daughters of genteel families in reduced circumstances to prosperous humble immigrants from Spain took place, the common effect was to produce rancorous antipathies which turned children against parents and cousin against cousin.

If upper-class Spaniards from the Peninsula often gained material and social advantages by favoritism and nepotism, and humbler representatives of the master race prospered through diligence and the better opportunities of the New World, many individuals in both categories were less successful. These self-proclaimed *hidalgos,* who had not found fortune or favor with the powerful, were little disposed to remedy matters by exerting themselves in useful occupations. Their scorn of manual labor and of trades soon reduced them to roving vagabonds on the highways or to loafers, ne'er-do-wells, pickpockets, and the like on the streets and squares of the larger towns and cities—the New World *pícaros* of contemporary literary fame in Spain. These renegade Spaniards wandered about the countryside preying upon the browbeaten Indians and mixed elements, and it was their common practice to note some particularly desirable piece of land for a farm, ranch, or millsite held by an Indian community and report its existence to an influential official or member of the viceroy's retinue. The luckless natives were soon deprived of their property by forced sale at a mere pittance while the knavish Spaniards received an acceptable commission for their dubious services.

In the cities these disreputable whites often became leaders in the dark underworld of half-caste, Indian, and Negro criminals and perverts. Still other unregenerate Spaniards resembled outcasts later called "beachcombers." Both species were termed *zaramullos* in the seventeenth century, and a contemporary Mexican writer describes them as "knaves, rascals, and cape-snatchers [who], in falling away from their [white] allegiance, are the worst of all in such a vile rabble." The habitues of local dives and *pulquerías,* they were ever ready to incite the wretched Indians, Negroes, and miscegenated masses to riots and tumults, and take advantage of such upheavals to loot and plunder the shops and homes of countrymen.

The most profound and enduring cleavage among the dominant white classes was undoubtedly between those born in Spain and those born of Spanish parentage in America. The latter, called Creoles, had appeared on the New World scene before the sixteenth century conquistadors had finished their work, and within a generation they formed a well-defined type acutely sensitive and continually afflicted by feelings of inferiority. Though it is often asserted that the first conquerors, having left their wives at home in Spain, quickly consorted with women of the vanquished Indians and produced a hybrid race, it is clearly evident that white representatives of the feminine sex were by no means absent in the stormy days of conquest and early settlement. Hence, a generation of American-born Spaniards promptly emerged upon the scene to receive, in due course, the originally unflattering designation by which they are known.

The repressed feeling of this class, frequently exacerbated by the condescension of the Peninsulars, remained one of the most deep-seated of the Baroque tensions, afflicting colonial society, and ultimately it resulted in secession from the Spanish empire. The hated *gachupines,* as the European Spaniards were dubbed, deliberately excluded the Creoles from the higher and more remunerative offices of the viceregal State and Church, and permitted them only subordinate roles in their own government. This discrimination was, in part, a calculated policy of the Spanish crown which feared separatist tendencies in the overseas realms, and also, in part, because it needed to appease importunate office-seekers swarming about the royal Court at Madrid. It rationalized this injustice by embracing the popular belief that the climate and environment of the New World had an enervating effect on children born of Europeans there. These offspring, it was assumed, matured early in a sort of "rotten ripe" fashion, and quickly entered upon a physical and mental decline which, of course, clearly disqualified them for the heavy responsibilities of high office. Few, indeed, were the American-born whites appointed viceroys, archbishops, and judges of the higher tribunals during the three colonial centuries.

This situation was naturally galling to the Creole, in the veins of whom flowed the undiluted blood of the proud hidalgo and often that of the first conquerors and settlers, and this imputed inferiority filled him with a loathing of the *gachupines* that he was compelled to veil. Denied an outlet for his talents and energies in his own government, and endowed with a fierce pride that regarded the countinghouse and factory as beneath the dignity of a gentleman, he too often turned to a life of indolence and outright vice. Frequently a member of the landowning aristocracy, he preferred to live as an absentee proprietor in the cities and larger towns where his vanity was equalled by his lofty ignorance. Other Creoles, who were virtually landless, strove to keep up the appearances and arrogance of the well-to-do. Thomas Gage[1] described one of

[1] ED. NOTE: An English friar who went to Mexico and Middle America during the first half of the seventeenth century, traveling widely before returning to renounce his vows and become a Puritan preacher. Later he described his travels in the book, *A New Survey of the West Indies,* published in 1648, which is highly critical of Spain in America.

these types whom he professed to have seen in Chiapas, a southern province of Mexico, but it would seem that his inspiration was the pathetically vain Squire portrayed in the famous Spanish picaresque tale, *Lazarillo de Tormes.*

And thus, Reader, by this Don Melchor's wit and ability would I have thee judge of the gentlemen Creoles or natives of Chiapa; and yet as presumptuous they are and arrogant as if the noblest blood in the Court of Madrid ran through their veins. It is a common thing amongst them to make a dinner only with a dish of frijoles in black broth, boiled with pepper and garlic, saying it is the most nourishing meat in all Indies; and after this so stately a dinner they will be sure to come out to the street-door of their houses to see and to be seen, and there for half an hour will they stand shaking off the crumbs of bread from their clothes, bands (but especially from their ruffs when they use them) and from their mustachios. And with their toothpickers they will stand picking their teeth, as if some small partridge bone stuck in them; nay if a friend pass by at that time, they will be sure to find out some crumb or other in the mustachio. . . . and they will be sure to vent out some non-truth, as to say: Ah Señor que linda perdiz he comido hoy, "O Sir, what a dainty partridge have I eat today," whereas they pick out nothing from their teeth but a black husk of a dry frijole or Turkey bean.

Open to this Creole class were the professions of law, medicine and theology, but the majority was temperamentally unsuited to sustained intellectual effort and its ample leisure was rarely productive of more than a certain dilettantism and an unrestrained flow of bombastic verse. The neo-scholasticism of the Baroque age stimulated the shallow erudition and hollow verbalism in which some members of this group sought a compensatory superiority. But few escaped a deepening sense of frustration and a festering dislike of their fellowmen of whatever race or color.

Another sector of this neomedieval society, predominantly white though including persons of mixed blood and even Indians, was the clergy. Since the sixteenth century Conquest this ecclesiastical element had increased rapidly in number and influence as the Church grew more wealthy and powerful. The continued presence of a large body of pagan and half-Christianized natives appeared to justify the ever-enlarging staff of clergymen until, by the seventeenth century, they constituted a considerable fraction of the population. The Church's forces were divided into the secular priests entrusted with administering the Sacraments and preventing backsliding among the faithful, and the religious orders such as the Franciscans, Dominicans, Augustinians, Jesuits, and the like, upon whom devolved primarily the tasks of education and proselyting among the heathen. As the crusading fervor of the Conquest died away and as more settled conditions prevailed jurisdictional disputes and doctrinal differences tended to replace the earlier zeal of both groups of clergymen. The acquisition of lands and the existence of a labor supply in the docile neophytes and the Indian peasantry rapidly increased the Church's wealth, and multiplying monasteries and convents dotted the land, particularly in the more populous areas. These institutions in turn drew off a growing number of men and women from more productive pursuits and attracted a steady stream of clergymen from Spain, usually to the higher levels of the hierarchy. The number of priests, monks, and nuns became disproportionate to the needs of the New World society and a heavy drain upon its resources. Inevitably, the weight of this burden fell hardest upon the exploited Indian population.

When Fray García Guerra ruled as Archbishop-Viceroy of Mexico the Franciscans were said to maintain one hundred and seventy-two monasteries and religious houses, the Augustinians ninety, and the Dominicans sixty-nine, to which were added those of the various other orders. In 1611 the excessive number of these establishments moved the Pope, Paul V, to issue a bull suppressing convents not occupied by at least eight friars, but little respect greeted this papal decree. Many of these institutions amassed large properties in lands and goods which enabled them to conduct highly profitable business ventures of a capitalistic character. It was this wealth that made possible the Baroque splendor of so many ecclesiastical edifices and the luxurious manner of living for so many of the expanding membership of the orders. These circumstances inevitably brought in their train a relaxation of monastic ideals, rules, and morals, notorious in the Baroque age and later.

It is, perhaps, a little questionable to summon again the apostate Thomas Gage to give evidence on conditions in seventeenth century Mexico, particularly on matters relating to clergymen, yet his *New Survey of the West Indies* contains much truth. In relating his journey inland from Vera Cruz around 1625 he professes to be shocked by the gambling, drinking, and the profanity of the mendicant friars in the Franciscan monastery at Jalapa where he was a temporary guest. Especially horrifying to him was the hypocrisy of a monk playing cards with his confreres. "Though formerly he had touched money," wrote the scandalized Gage,

and with his fingers had laid it to the stake on the table, yet sometimes to make the company laugh, if he had chanced to win a double vie . . . then would he take the end of one sleeve of his habit and open wide the other broad sleeve, saying: I have vowed not to touch money, nor keep any . . . but my sleeve may touch it, and my sleeve may keep it.

The Baroque age witnessed much constructive missionary activity on the frontiers of New Spain and in the founding of schools; still other endeavors testified to the zeal of the clergy. Unhappily these positive contributions were more than counterbalanced by a moral laxity and a parasitism afflicting many religious establishments. Throughout Spanish America, as in Spain itself, the rules of many monastic orders so far relaxed that numerous members lived outside convent walls and maintained illegal families and dependents in private houses. Nunneries offered commodious refuge for large numbers of unmarriageable daughters who spent their lives in comfortable cells surrounded by conveniences and attended by personal servants and slaves. This idleness was not always conducive to the expected decorum, and permanent confinement sometimes brought antipathies into the open. Friction between inmates hailing from different provinces of Spain, between Peninsulars and Creoles, and between representatives of varied social classes not infrequently produced enough heat to flame into unseemly disturbances, and the quarrels over the election of priors and superiors often assumed such violent proportions that secular authorities of the State found it necessary to intervene. Particularly vexatious for the viceroys and their coadjutors were the rivalries of the religious orders who, with little of the otherworldly piety and concern suggested by their vows, jockeyed for power and preference in the affairs of the universities and even in more political agencies.

Still other human elements entered the white composite, increasing its diversity. Too readily is it assumed that the restrictive policies of the Spanish crown limited emigration to the colonies to approved nationals and excluded other Europeans. Records of licenses and permits issued to passengers embarking for the Indies plainly reveal the presence of Italians, Flemings, Germans, Austrians, Greeks, Irishmen, and even Dutchmen, and Englishmen on Atlantic crossings of the merchant ships and galleons. As the Spanish Empire decayed, leaving its overseas possessions more vulnerable to piratical attacks, the king's ministers authorized the sending of skilled artisans, metallurgists, engineers, and other technicians, most of whom were aliens, to modernize fortifications and improve mining and other industries. Similarly, Italians, Flemings, Frenchmen and others, apparently more zealous for martyrdom in the frontier missions than either the Spanish or Creole clergymen, were subsidized for this purpose and sent to America. Spain's restrictive policy with respect to emigration stemmed from a religious rather than an antiforeign bias. Its essential requirement was that non-Spanish Europeans be orthodox Catholics.

If the number of authorized foreigners was fairly considerable, those entering without credentials of any sort were probably more numerous. Seaports such as Vera Cruz invariably harbored subjects of other nations who had deserted their ships, or were left by passing vessels. Though Spanish captains were severely enjoined to carry no unlicensed crewmen or passengers, and port officials were cautioned to prevent illegal entries, many undesirables, like forbidden books, found their way past these barriers and into the interior of the viceroyalties. Though now and then the net of the police-minded Inquisition ensnared them, many more remained inconspicuous in the heterogeneous population. Those who lingered in the seaports sometimes found themselves impressed as sailors in the returning fleets or in maritime expeditions fitted out for explorations.

Such extraneous elements were not always of European origin. Between the West Coast port of Acapulco and Manila in the Philippine Islands a freight and passenger service lasted for nearly two and a half centuries. The annual galleons plowing their tortuous course across the vast Pacific injected a slight admixture of Asiatic blood into the ethnic complexity of the Baroque society of Old Mexico. These clumsy crafts, sometimes the largest ships of the time, carried crews of Filipinos, Malays, and Chinese who, if they survived the arduous voyage of six or more months, settled somewhere along the coast or drifted into the interior to mingle with the varied inhabitants. Some brought technical skills useful to the economy. In commenting on the exquisite workmanship of the goldsmiths, Thomas Gage reports that: "The Indians, and the people of China that have been made Christians and every year come thither, have perfected the Spaniards in that trade."

At the opposite extreme of the ethnic spectrum appeared the Negroes who, from the Conquest itself, had played an active role in the military and economic subjugation of the land. From the outset the Spaniards had displayed an enthusiasm for wealth with a minimum of labor and, as the Indians of the West Indies proved unsatisfactory workers, African slavery was introduced almost at once. Around 1441 the Portuguese had begun this traffic in human beings during their explorations along the Dark Continent, but it scarcely seemed likely to develop into a large-scale operation. The discovery of America and the opportunity offered by its rich soil to satisfy the newly whetted sweet-tooth of Europe by sugar cultivation soon placed a premium on Negro field hands. Even before the death of the discoverer of the New World the Spanish governor of the island of Hispaniola begged that no more Africans be shipped because many were escaping into the hills and joining the Indians. Thus, almost coincident with the advent of the blackman in the colonies, arose a menace that endured until final emancipation. These fugitive slaves, called *cimarrones,* reverted to their tribal ways, formed wilderness communities, and preyed upon the white man's commerce.

The high mortality of West Indian workers in the mines and on the plantations made the governor's protest ineffective and by 1510 the traffic had increased. Eight years later the Spanish crown permitted the shipping of 4,000 Negroes to the Caribbean area, and by 1540 some 10,000 were imported annually into the mainland; by the seventeenth century the total each year probably reached 75,000. The year 1522 saw the first recorded Negro insurrection when twenty blacks owned by Diego Columbus, son of the Discoverer, revolted and killed several of the outnumbered Spaniards on Hispaniola. But, almost at the same time, Africans were accompanying the conquistadors on their conquests of Mexico and Peru as burden-bearers. In April, 1533, the Spanish king received word that, within five months, more than six hundred whites and four hundred black bondsmen had passed through Panama en route to the former empire of the Incas, and Cortés' restless lieutenant, Alvarado, also led an army to Quito in present-day Ecuador which included two hundred Negro servitors. As centers of wealth and luxury developed in Mexico and elsewhere, Africans became domestic servants and found their way into crafts and trades. More enterprising, in general, than the fatalistic Indians, they practiced ingenious forms of racketeering on the dominant classes in the cities and large towns where they congregated in such numbers as to cause profound anxiety among the white overlords. But their economic contribution was great and their labor provided the base of many fortunes made by their masters. The Negro's talent for organization and leadership occasionally brought comparative prominence, while his gifts enriched the arts of music, dance, folklore, sculpture, and carving.

Like the whites, the Negro also offered variations in the human spectrum of a Baroque society. Just as the Europeans presented shades from the alabaster whiteness of some Spanish women to the dark swarthiness of peninsular southerners, so the African varied from jet black to the lighter tints of *café au lait.* Slave trading activities had extended from the Senegal and Gambia rivers of the African west coast to Guinea to the eastward and south to Angola, and the traders took captives from the Ashanti, Fanti, Minas, and Dahomean tribes of the Gold Coast and the Yoruba of Nigeria. These Negroes differed as much among themselves in temperament, skills, language, and pigmentation as did the whites, and among them existed vague castes of an undefined pattern.

The third racial group, the Indian, was, of course, of fundamental importance sociologically. Despite recurring plagues and harsh exploitation which, in the early seventeenth century, had severely reduced the aboriginal population, it far outnumbered that of the Europeans. While the social structure of the remarkably advanced civilizations encountered by the Spaniards was largely crushed under the weight of the Conquest, representatives of the Indian nobility did retain some feudal rights and enjoyed a certain eminence. In the more thickly populated districts of the south, members of the conquered race were prosperous merchants. In this region Thomas Gage reports that:

. . . Indians live there who traffic to Mexico [City] and about the country with twenty or thirty mules of their own, chopping and changing, buying and selling commodities, and some of them are thought to be worth ten, or twelve, or fifteen thousand ducats, which is much for an Indian to get among the Spaniards . . .

He also describes a rich Indian in Chiapas with a title of Don, a fine stable of horses, and a mode of living as ostentatious as a Spaniard, who served as governor of a town. But the lot of most Indians was clearly much less fortunate. Their status as a subjugated people tended to compress individual differences into a faceless mass and reduce them to a collective serfdom. Their sedentary nature included a certain passivity and fatalism which facilitated Spanish control and perpetuated a feudal relationship between conquerors and conquered, but these qualities enabled the Indians to preserve many of their characteristics which subtly affected the culture imposed upon them. Their artistic instinct served to enrich the complex patterns of Baroque expression, quietly imbuing them with a character distinct from the contemporary manifestations in Spain and, perhaps, accounting for the longer duration of this intricate style in Mexico and Spanish America generally.

On the outermost fringes of Spanish settlement roamed nomadic war-like tribes little disposed to abandon a wild, free manner of living. Foiled in the efforts to vanquish these barbarous aborigines by swift, dramatic conquest, the Spaniards were obliged to engage in sporadic guerrilla warfare with these elusive foes. It was particularly aggravating because this resistance excluded the whites from regions which, though uninvitingly arid, might still fulfill their dreams of rich mines and sudden wealth. Courageous friars, with less materialistic motives, penetrated this forbidding hinterland to establish missions and reduce these fierce tribes to a Christian way of life. The seventeenth century witnessed heroic efforts of this sort in the far north and west, in New Mexico, Arizona, Lower California, Sinaloa and Sonora, but success was limited and the effect on the older settlements was negligible.

Where the ethnic pattern of colonial society acquired its most Baroque complexity was among its components of mixed blood. The association of white, red, and black races soon produced a strange conglomerate of humanity which included entirely new species of *homo sapiens*. This miscegenation coincided with the Conquest itself in the basic fusions of European and Indian, European and Negro, and Indian and Negro. By the time that the consolidation of Spanish civilization was giving the populous centers of New Spain a distinct character—and this was clearly visible by the end of the sixteenth century—the progressive mixing of diverse elements had created a veritable kaleidoscope of shades, complexions, and social castes. As time went on the pattern of old and new species became labyrinthine, almost defying analysis and forming a unique composite of human types, pigments, and psychology.

The generally enlightened laws promulgated by the Spanish crown took cognizance of this racial amalgamation by recognizing as prototypes the mestizos, offspring of Indian and white mating, mulattoes, and the *zambaigos* or *zambos,* as the products of Indian and Negro unions were called. But these were, of course, merely rudimentary combinations, and the lawmakers found the ensuing mixtures a bewildering problem of classification. Successive generations of crossbreeding created a confusing maze and a baffling system of nomenclature to identify each variation. Literally scores of designations were invented or applied to the different gradations of color and blood whose varieties taxed the resources of the language. Most of the names were based on shades of complexion, but other anatomical features, such as the shape of the nose, thickness or thinness of lips, body structure and the like, furnished inspiration. Since these appellations were mostly bestowed by the dominant white castes they were intended to be humorous or downright insulting. The progeny of a *mestizo* couple, for example, was commonly called *tente en el aire* (suspended in the air), chiefly because it indicated no advance toward the white ancestry or no retrogression, as it was conceived, toward the Indian blood. If a *mestiza* woman married an Indian, the offspring might be called a *salta atrás* (a throwback) because the trend was toward the less-esteemed indigenous progenitor.

In the more intricate fluctuations of such advances and retreats of a mongrel population, and especially in mixtures in which Indian and Negro blood was dominant, the names bore connotations of scorn, contempt, mockery, and sneers. *No te entiendo* (I don't get you), for example, was the offspring of a *tente en el aire* and a mulatto woman, while an *Ahí te estás* (there you are) was the child of a *mestiza* mother and a *coyote* father, who, in turn, was the product of the union of a *mestizo* and an Indian. Appellations of a zoological origin were deliberately derogatory such as: mule, coyote, wolf, cow, and the like. Each country, and even regions, had names of its own for the multitudinous mixtures, and a given designation might be used for a different combination of genes. The heterogeneous nature of this large segment of society is abundantly clear, a condition accentuated by a confusing array of castes into which it divided. Mutual jealousy and lack of cohesion kept this proletarian mass asunder as similar negative impulses did the more privileged groups, which fact largely explains why the restiveness of these overseas subjects of Spain, occasionally evident, was not translated for centuries into active opposition to the crown's authority.

Social position, based mainly on white blood, determined to a considerable extent the occupation of the individual in the more genteel pursuits, with idleness preferred, particularly in Creole circles. The large hybrid population, with its own complex hierarchy, had callings suited to its varying status. The upper strata with preponderant white blood were scarcely distinguishable from the Creoles or humbler Europeans and might pass as such; the lower approached the lowly condition of the Indians and Negroes and shared much the same destiny. The *mestizo* tended to find a place at the top of the mixed groups; in the sixteenth century the Spaniards accorded him paternal treatment. As his number increased a larger measure of discrimination was his lot—this prejudice often sprang from his "illegitimacy" and was more political and economic than ethnical. It was, perhaps, a by-product of the hostile feeling in Spain for the remaining *Moriscos*[2] and the mistrust of the so-called "new Christians" common in the days of the Counter Reformation. The military profession still remained one of the most honored in the contemporary culture, and the *mestizo* could find a place in it. The term "Spaniards," so frequently used in the reports of campaigns against pirates and the Indians on the frontiers, mostly referred to persons of diluted white blood. The trades and crafts were also open to this group, though usually the more menial tasks. The Indians were early taught such practical pursuits and might engage in these activities as well but, in the main, like the Negroes, they found themselves in the *obrajes* or the sweatshops of textile manufacture, in domestic service, or condemned to the hard work of agriculture and the heavy labor of the mines—slaves in fact though not in theory.

The misery and utter ignorance of this variegated and exploited proletariat were extreme. Their neglect and superstition made them a ready prey to a swarm of sorcerers and quacks who practiced magic rites and the black arts inherited from African and Indian barbarism. Faith in witchcraft, illuminati, animism, omens, charms, astrology, and the occult flourished in all castes and classes, including the dominant whites.

[2] ED. NOTE: Moors converted to Christianity.

Baroque, indeed, does this profusion of ethnological detail, intricate hierarchy, and superstitious credulity of a New World society appear in retrospect during the "long siesta of the seventeenth century"!

An Experiment in "Feudalism": French Canada in the Seventeenth Century

SIGMUND DIAMOND

The society of French Canada, hierarchical like that of Mexico, but less vital and, paradoxically, more fluid, is described in the following passage by Sigmund Diamond, professor of sociology at Columbia University. With perceptive insights developed by a long-time devotion to comparative study, he has analyzed the social organization of New France in the seventeenth century. Like McRae in an earlier selection, Diamond sees French Canada as an experiment in social planning within the framework of law, attitudes, economic institutions, and tradition. But doomed both by the realities of the Canadian environment and the unreality of royal policy, the attempt failed and there emerged instead a society often feudal in form, but something quite different in practice. Modifications designed to protect the original scheme, Diamond shows, fatally undermined it—perhaps the inevitable result of planning from a distance.

Certainly the French story differs sharply from that of Spain, which more effectively extended European institutions into the New World, or of England, which allowed the colonies to grow virtually in their own way. One has only to assess the role of the clergy or the king to realize this fact. In the Spanish colonies, for example, the secular clergy was far more effective as a unifying, Europeanizing factor than the priests of the French colonies. Moreover, in

From Sigmund Diamond, "An Experiment in 'Feudalism': French Canada in the Seventeenth Century," *William and Mary Quarterly*, 3rd Series, XVIII (January, 1961), 3-21, 33-34. Reprinted by permission of the author.

French America the king's efforts to impose his will were almost a complete failure, partially the result of his unyielding attitude toward the colonials. In Spanish America the monarch made the same effort but was more successful because of his willingness to compromise, to share public power with overseas settlers, and to tolerate colonial adaptations of policies imposed at home.

Of the three societies under scrutiny, only Canada did not employ slave labor on a large scale, although the French introduced slaves in large numbers in their Caribbean possessions. Like the English colonists, the French in Canada made no attempt to integrate Indians into the social order by consigning them (like the Spanish in Mexico and Peru) to a low rung on the social ladder, but instead segregated them in the wilderness and allowed them no place whatsoever in the colonial social structure. The absence of large Negro and Indian segments had important implications for Canadian society. In addition to those indicated in Diamond's essay, one may note particularly the homogeneity of French Canada and the absence of that bewildering profusion or racial mixtures which gave Mexico its texture and tensions, and yet, as Irving Leonard has argued, its stability.

I

T HE HISTORY OF SIXTEENTH- AND SEVENTEENTH-CENTURY COLONI-
zation provides an almost unique opportunity for the study of certain problems in social organization. The very requirement, as in the case of the British and French in North America, to establish settlements "where none before hath stood," or, as in the case of the Spanish in Central and South America, to devise a mode of accommodation with pre-existing societies, imposed the necessity of considering problems of social organization with a clarity and directness rarely before achieved. Nor was this entirely a matter of necessity. The creation of new societies raised thought about appropriate forms of organization to a new level of consciousness, not only because the situation created the need, but also because it created the opportunity. Man had now the possibility, so at least it seemed, of making a fresh beginning. Was it really necessary that he be forever burdened with the residue of the iniquity and folly of past history? Was it not possible to devise a new form of social organization in which at least some of the less desirable characteristics of the old would be eliminated? From consciousness of both necessity and opportunity came the impetus to create forms of social organization appropriate to achieve the ends held by the leaders of colonization ventures—whether corporations, private individuals invested with almost regal authority, or the crown.

How were the members of the new societies to be recruited? How were they to be motivated to accept the obligations attached to their positions in these new societies? How was order to be maintained between persons of different statuses? What should be the proper balance among ethic, reward, and sanction in getting persons to behave in the proper fashion? Would the family detach persons from their loyalty to the colonizing organization, or would it increase their satisfaction with their lot in the New World? What special features of social organization would have to be created to accommodate the new societies to sponsorship by joint-stock companies, and how might these be different in colonies undertaken by individuals or by government?

Simply to state these questions is to suggest that implicit in the history of early modern colonization is the problem of planned social action, and that this history may be re-examined with the view in mind of analyzing the discrepancy between the plan for the new society and the actual outcome of the effort to apply the plan. If, as appears to be the case, the effort to plan certain aspects of a social system may have unanticipated effects elsewhere in the system—effects that may negate the very purposes of the planners—an examination of the sources of these unanticipated effects may reveal to us more than we now know of the ways in which the different parts of a society are related, and how that society worked.

II

In New France, as in Virginia, the first persistent instrument used to achieve the purposes of colonization was the chartered commercial company. Society was brought to both Jamestown and Quebec in the ships of a commercial company, in both cases for the same reasons and with much the same consequences. The form of organization devised by the company proved incapable not only of balancing the somewhat contradictory objectives of the merchants—and others—who invested and the government which patronized, but even of solving the strictly business problem of recruiting the supplies of capital and labor necessary for the survival of the company. To take but one example, the great Company of One Hundred Associates, the most prominent of several that failed in New France before 1663, undertook by the terms of its charter to transport four thousand settlers between 1627 and 1642. It was, however, unable to devise a form of social organization that could reconcile its own interests in deploying its labor force into the most profitable economic pursuits with the interests of the government in fixing immigrants to the land and in establishing a polity, and with the interests of the population in receiving as many as possible of the rewards for under-

taking the hazardous task of bringing society to a wilderness. Colonization under commercial auspices was considered a failure, and with the
demise of the company in 1663, it devolved upon the government in
France, as it had upon the government in England in the case of the
Virginia Company in 1624, to create a more adequate form of social
organization. The cost of recruiting a population, of supplying it, of
motivating it to work, of defending it against its enemies became a
charge upon government and not upon private business.

What followed was a remarkable experiment in creating a society
according to plan, an attempt to utilize existing institutions—religion,
family, land tenure, law—and to adapt them, under government auspices, to the objectives of the planners and the needs of an immigrant
population under frontier conditions. The administrative demands entailed in such an effort were staggering. Hundreds of manuscript volumes
of home and colonial decrees and an even larger mass of correspondence, court decisions, and other official documents stand today as mute
testimony to the scope of the attempt. What, above all, characterizes the
plan is that it bore so clearly the stamp of that passion for rationality—
the desire to achieve order, symmetry, and harmony—which is the hall-
mark of bureaucratic endeavor. It would be anachronistic and yet truth-
ful to describe the objective of the French authorities in Canada after
1663, not as the creation of a society to be governed by political means,
but as the creation of an administrative system in which persons would
have fixed positions in a table of organization, would behave in the way
deemed appropriate for those positions, and would be manipulated, de-
ployed, and disciplined by measures more compatible with the requirements of a formal organization than of a society.

To a degree, of course, this desire to rationalize the operations of the
system of governance was already highly developed in France. The attempt of the seigniors of the *ancien régime* to bring order into their own
economic activities and into their relations with tenants is by now well
known; even better known is the celebrated effort of the monarchy under
Louis XIV and his successors to reform the system of administration.
What permitted the same effort to be carried even further in Canada was
the possibility of beginning at the beginning. Where a society did not
already exist, there was no necessity to make the best of a bad situation,
to compromise the goal of rationality by having to reckon with the need
to adjust to established institutions and traditions.

Instructing the Dauphin in the desirability of recruiting only persons
of moderate social position into the civil service, Louis XIV wrote: "It
was not to my interest to select subjects of higher degree. It was important that they should not conceive hopes any higher than it pleased me to

grant them, something which is difficult among persons of high birth."
The tendency betrayed by the King's instructions to regard his civil
servants as instruments to aid him in achieving his own purposes had
an even wider extension in Canada, for there everyone was looked upon
as the King viewed his civil servant, as an agent of the state. The letter of
Jean Baptiste Colbert[1] to Marquis Prouville de Tracy upon the latter's
assumption of the governorship is exceptional only because Tracy's position in the administration imposed the necessity of greater explicitness.
"The first thing that I must insist upon," wrote Colbert, "is that, since the
king takes note of all of his affairs, you must address yourself directly to
him in making reports and receiving his orders. It would be well for you
to observe this in the future, for although I inform him of everything
written to me, those, like you, who hold positions of trust ought to have
it as a maxim to have their main relationship with His Majesty."

Relying upon the loyalty of their direct subordinates and the self-
discipline of the population, the metropolitan authorities aimed at the
creation of a society in Canada in which the vast majority of persons
would be firmly fixed to the land, would live peaceably in their villages,
and would respond obediently to the commands of their superiors. The
reins of legitimate power were held firmly in the hands of the administrative authorities and their designated surrogates, and any tendency toward
the development of competing authority, even when it conformed to
practices already established in France, was rigorously suppressed.

Every aspect of life in Canada was subject to rational calculation and
was alterable by purposeful action. Political institutions, the family, Indian affairs, the range of permissible trades and occupations, the amount
of prestige and honor to be associated with each status in the society
were all carefully regulated. The behavior of each major segment of the
population was prescribed in the minutest detail, even to the point of
regulating the order of precedence in religious and secular ceremonies,
the appropriate forms of address, and the types of weapons that each
might bear. The total corpus of these regulations betrays the assumption,
central to the conception of the administrator, that each person is essentially the occupant of a position in an organization and that his behavior
can be made to conform to the needs of the system for order and
stability.

Precautions were taken that nothing should interfere with the flow of
authority in the established chain of command. Though occasional meetings of the population were held to discuss problems and to hear proposed programs, never did these assume the character of representative

[1] ED. NOTE: Jean Baptiste Colbert (1619-1683), Louis XIV's indefatigable
finance minister, who also directed colonial affairs while in office, 1661-1683.

assemblies; they were *ad hoc* bodies, summoned to listen and not to argue. When, elated by his own cleverness, Governor Louis de Buade, Comte de Frontenac, informed Colbert in 1672 that he had administered an oath of loyalty to the seigniors and, for convenience, to a group of habitants acting on behalf of all, he received a blistering reply.

Since our Kings have long regarded it as good for their service not to convoke the Estates-General of the Kingdom in order perhaps to abolish insensibly this ancient usage, you, on your part, should very rarely, or, to speak correctly, never, give a corporate form to the inhabitants of Canada. You should even, as the colony strengthens, suppress gradually the office of Syndic, who presents petitions in the name of the inhabitants, for it is well that each should speak for himself and no one for all.

Nothing was permitted to escape the hawklike eyes of those responsible for seeing that the colonists behaved according to plan, and no problem was too small to be taken to the highest official. Jérôme de Pontchartrain himself, the minister of colonies in Paris, was called upon to decide disputes involving a cow strayed into someone's garden, a brawl at a church door, the virtue of a certain lady. Colbert had to be informed, as evidence of the degree to which prescriptions for proper behavior were observed, that two captains had been married, one lieutenant engaged, and "four ensigns are in treaty with their mistresses, and are already half engaged." Jean Talon, struck with the thought that population increase might be achieved by the intermarriage of Indians and French, studied the reproductive capacity of Indian women and reported that it was impaired by their nursing children longer than necessary; but, he added, "this obstacle to the speedy building up of the colony can be overcome by a police regulation."

In short, what was planned was a society in which all persons would be under a jurisdiction and patronage that were at once French, royal, and orthodox. Stability would be guaranteed by each person's having a precise place and acting in accordance with the behavior defined as appropriate to that place. The elements of this society were, of course, diverse—government regulation of economic activity, a special system of land tenure, and elaborate code of law, and established church, royal patronage of the institution of the family—and every effort was made to weld them together into an organization in which discipline would be achieved because each man would remain loyal to the institutions to which he was attached.

The fur trade, which had been at once a blessing and a curse to the colony, was the subject of endless consideration by government officials. Although the form of regulation varied, the trade was controlled at virtually all times so as to restrict the number and influence of persons engaged in it. The privileged few were thus to be attached to the government with the ties of gratitude that flow from profit, while the mass of the population would not be diverted from the performance of necessary agricultural tasks. The *coureurs de bois* were to be quarantined so that their lawlessness could not contaminate what was hoped would be an obedient agricultural society. Men who desert the land to enter the forests, said Talon, are men, "without Christianity, without sacraments, without religion, without priests, without laws, without magistrates, sole masters of their own actions and of the application of their wills. . . ."

Population growth, recognized by government officials as indispensable to increasing agricultural production and, at least indirectly, to reducing the overhead costs of administering the colony, was promoted through immigration, encouragement of marriage, family subsidies, and attempts to mobilize the Indians into the labor force. The policy of "Francisation," which included conversion, domiciliation, intermarriage, and education of the Indians in the ways of the white man, was undertaken in the hope that, made tractable by their re-education, they would swell the labor force. It quickly became evident that the policy had failed, and that population growth would have to come about through immigration and natural increase.

In 1668 Colbert suggested to Talon that those "who may seem to have absolutely renounced marriage should be made to have additional burdens, and be excluded from all honors; it would be well even to add some marks of infamy." The Intendant was quick to take the hint; bachelors were barred from the right to hunt, fish, trade with the Indians, and even to enter the woods. By act of the Sovereign Council of Canada, "any inhabitant having in legitimate marriage ten living children, not priests, *religieux* or *religieuses* shall be paid three hundred livres a year, and those who have twelve shall be paid four hundred livres a year." Young men who married before the age of twenty were given a bonus. Fathers whose sons were not married by the age of twenty or whose daughters were still vestals at the age of sixteen were to be fined and summoned to the court every six months.

But to encourage marriage the government would have to take the initiative in providing women, unless it were willing—which it was not—to tolerate "a thousand disorders in the settlements . . . where the women are very glad to have several husbands and where the men cannot get even one wife." Marriage, it was anticipated, would not only increase the birth rate but would lead to a more settled and orderly life. As in Virginia, therefore, the government assumed the responsibility of shipping from France "demoiselles" for the military officers and what pious Mother Marie de l'Incarnation called "une marchandise mêlée"—mixed goods—for the ordinary settlers, something more than a thousand altogether.

Still, French Canada's population growth, dependent overwhelmingly upon natural increase and very little upon immigration, lagged far behind that of the British North American colonies and even behind Canadian requirements. As late as 1710 Governor Philippe de Rigaud, Marquis de Vaudreuil, complained that there was not enough labor for the seigniors to cultivate even half their estates; six years later he was recommending that condemned salt-smugglers in France be shipped as indentured servants at the expense of the farmers-general. In 1733 Governor Charles de la Boische, Marquis de Beauharnois, and Intendant Gilles Hocquart echoed the complaint: "The scarcity of men, and the high wages of both agricultural and urban labor, considerably diminishes the revenues of landlords and merchants." Despite every effort of a government that exhorted and a people that produced, the population of French Canada amounted to only about 5 per cent of the population south of the St. Lawrence River by the middle of the eighteenth century.

But neither government regulation nor family attachments were, in the view of the French authorities, sufficient to maintain social discipline; religion, too, was counted on to disseminate an ethic calculated to remind each man to keep to his allotted place. From the beginning of New France, the Roman Catholic Church was given major responsibility for enforcing the ban on Protestants in Canada, and the zealousness with which it responded to the task of rooting out unorthodoxy in both its Jansenist and Protestant forms revealed that secular as well as religious discipline was its proper concern. The importance of orthodoxy from the religious viewpoint was self-evident. "On the side of the state," wrote Bishop François Xavier de Laval, "it appears to be no less important. Everyone knows that Protestants in general are not so attached to His Majesty as Catholics. . . . To multiply the number of Protestants in Canada would be to give occasion for the outbreak of revolutions."

Doctrinal conflict was minimized, therefore, by screening prospective immigrants, but the church played a no less significant role in disciplining colonists once they had arrived. The keynote was sounded in a letter from Louis XIV to Bishop Laval: "As I have been informed of your continued care to hold the people in their duty towards God and towards me by the good education you give or cause to be given to the young, I write this letter to express my satisfaction with conduct so salutary, and to exhort you to persevere in it." The nature of this education may be inferred from the list of virtues commended to boys, drawn from the rulebook of the Petit Séminaire in Quebec: "humility, obedience, purity, meekness, modesty, simplicity, chastity, charity, and an ardent love of Jesus and his Holy Mother." All schools but one were under control of the church, and that single exception—the School of Mathematics and Hydrography—passed under its influence early in the eighteenth century.

In its role as custodian of morals and, though its pretensions in this area were disputed, of law, the church went even further. It regulated the style of clothing; it censored books; it established with meticulous accuracy the order of priority of both religious and secular officials on ceremonial occasions; it attacked usury and supported its attack by refusing confession to usurers; it shipped back to France immoral men, including those who were so unmindful of their situation in life as to fall in love with more highly placed girls; and it attempted to cultivate an ethic of obligation and obedience, of simplicity and austerity.

Most important of all, however, it threw the weight of ecclesiastical discipline behind the effort to fix the population·into assigned positions; the sanction of excommunication itself was invoked against those who left the land without permission and traded illegally for furs with the Indians. Although there were disputes between secular and religious officials when either tried to exercise authority that pinched the other, they were as one in recognizing the importance of the church in disciplining the inferiors of both, in urging upon them acceptance of a code of beliefs that would confine their behavior within the limits desired by higher authority. We must "multiply the number of parishes and . . . render them fixed . . . ," wrote Governor Jacques-René de Brissay, Marquis de Denonville, to Colbert in 1685. "This undertaking . . . would be a sure means of establishing schools, with which the *curés* would occupy themselves and thus accustom the children at an early hour to control themselves and become useful." Finally, in its capacity as landowner, the church assumed the role of model seignior, and attempted by the force of its own example to influence the behavior of other landlords. By 1750 the church held over two million arpents[2] of land, more than one-third of all the grants that had been made.

But the most characteristic institution of the old regime in Canada—the one that gave tone to the entire society—was the seigniorial system. There was much in it that was reminiscent of medieval feudalism, but only reminiscent. Feudalism in France was an organic growth; in Canada it was a transplanted institution, and the French administration saw to it that in the transplanting it was pruned of less desirable characteristics. The French monarchy had established itself in the teeth of feudal

[2] ED. NOTE: An arpent of Paris is equal to about five-sixths of an English acre.

opposition and was in no mood now to offer the seigniors sufficient independence and power so as to require repetition of the experience. When Governor Tracy and Intendant Talon drew up their "Project de Règlement" in 1667, they warned that since

. . . obedience and fidelity [two words obscured] are more likely to suffer attenuation in distant provinces of the state than in the neighbors of the Sovereign Authority, which resides mainly in the person of the prince and has more force and virtue there than in any other person, it is the part of prudence to prevent in the establishment of the growing state of Canada all those vexatious revolutions which might render it monarchical, aristocratic, or democratic, or even—by a balanced power and authority between subjects—divide it into parts and give rise to such a dismemberment as France suffered by the creation of such sovereignties within the Kingdom as Soissons, Orleans, Champagne, and others.

In their concern lies the clue to the essential difference between French and Canadian feudalism. The landed seignior in Canada was entitled to many of the rights possessed by his counterpart in France—potential membership in the nobility; ceremonial rights like fealty and homage; judicial rights like holding private courts; and more lucrative rights such as the collection of rents and mutation fines, the imposition of labor services, and the monopoly of all milling—and the enforcement of these rights was presumably guaranteed by the extension to Canada of the law code known as the Custom of Paris and the beneficent protection of the royal authority. Nevertheless, the position of the Canadian seignior was far different from that of the French.

The right to have a private court was his, but the use of the term *haute, moyenne, et basse justice* in Canada must not delude us into thinking that it held the same meaning as in France. The existence of the competing royal court eventually limited private jurisdiction to relatively simple cases about seigniorial dues and obligations, and even in these the habitant had free right of appeal to the royal court. Nor were the profits of justice as lucrative in Canada as in France; where population was sparse, the opportunity to squeeze income from it in the courts was limited by the small number of cases and by the fear that too much repression would cause the seignior's labor force to move to the lands of a less exacting landlord. "I will not say that the Goddess of Justice is more chaste and impartial here than in France," wrote Baron Louis Armand de la Hontan, "but at any rate, if she is sold, she is sold more cheaply." In Canada the problem was not so much to check the encroachments of the seigniorial courts as to force the reluctant seigniors to accept the profitless and limited jurisdiction the Crown imposed on them.

So, too, the seigniors of Canada had the rights of *banalité* and *corvée.* Under conditions of severely limited population, however, these were drained of most of their significance. The intendants of Canada, conscious of the fact that onerous obligations on the peasantry would hamper immigration, restricted the size of the payments to the seigniors and forced them to improve their mills. So profitless were these rights that, as with private courts, the problem was not so much to control their abuse as to get the seigniors to exercise them at all. In 1686 a royal decree was issued requiring the seigniors to build mills on their land grants on penalty of losing their monopoly, but for twenty years the seigniors sabotaged enforcement of the decree by not promulgating it. What under other circumstances would have been a profitable privilege was for the Canadian seignior a burdensome cost.

Even the conditions under which he held land and could legitimately demand payments from his sub-infeudees were different from those in France. Squirm though he might, never could the seignior wholly evade the scrutiny of the intendants, who were determined to prevent the payments owed by the *censitaires,* the peasants, from becoming too burdensome. Even more, his power to dispose of his own domain was limited in such a way as to reduce his maneuverability and to make him essentially an agent of the Crown in the achievement of its purposes. After several preliminary gestures, the King, through the Arrêts of Marly in 1711, decreed that all seigniorial grants not settled and developed through subinfeudation would revert to the Crown, and that the payments to seigniors from subinfeudated lands must be uniform and limited. In the minds of the administrators, the seigniors were less proprietors than trustees, entitled to occupy the land only if they performed the essential tasks required of them.

Though the Canadian seignior was sometimes able to evade some of the restrictions imposed upon him, there can be little doubt that his rights were more limited than were those of the French. Still, they were believed sufficient to get him to assume the tasks for which the Crown held him responsible—to clear the land, to settle it with farmers, to support the church and the state, and to keep his subordinates in their places. For those who did their tasks well, there was the added incentive of possible ennoblement: We must grant titles, Talon told Colbert in 1670, to "fill the officers and richer seigniors with a new zeal for the settlement of their lands in hope of being recompensed with titles as well." Having deprived the seignior of many of the attributes that permitted him to be a seignior, the King's administrators yet hoped he would act like one.

As with the seigniors, so with the *censitaires.* They, too, had rights and obligations differing somewhat from their brothers' in France. They had to clear the land lest it revert to the seignior; they owed him rent and mutation fines; they worked for him and give him part of their catch of fish; they paid him deference; they were not allowed to engage in the fur trade. Yet, their duties were less onerous than in France, and they were protected from excessive exploitation by a solicitous officialdom. Besides, the prospect of improvement was such, so it was anticipated, as to induce them willingly to accept their position. "There are so many strong and robust peasants in France," wrote Father Paul le Jeune,

who have no bread to put in their mouths; is it possible they are so afraid of losing sight of the village steeple, as they say, that they would rather languish in their misery and poverty, than to place themselves some day at their ease among the inhabitants of New France, where with the blessings of earth they will more easily find those of heaven and of the soul?

In short, the seigniorial system in Canada was transformed by the authorities into an agency of land settlement, an instrument for peopling the country, and a mechanism for insuring social stability.

III

How did the system actually work? If long-term stability and social discipline were the objectives desired by the authorities, they were not the objectives attained.

The *sine qua non* of successful colonization was the mobilization of an adequate labor force. In Canada, as in British North America, experiments in the use of forced labor and of the local Indians failed, and it soon became necessary to recruit labor by voluntary means. To do so, however, such substantial concessions had to be made that the real position occupied by the labor force in the new society was utterly different not only from its position in Old World society but even from what the planners of the system had intended.

The companies before 1663 recognized the necessity of offering incentives, but sought to minimize them in an effort to keep costs low. Louis Hébert, the Paris apothecary who became the first settler at Quebec, had been offered full support for himself and his family for a period of two years plus two hundred crowns per year for three years as inducement to emigrate. After he arrived, however, the company imposed harsher terms: he was given only one hundred crowns per year; his entire family and his servant were required to work for the company for three years, after which time he was required to sell all his produce to the company at prices current in France; he could work on clearing his land and building his house only when the chief factor did not need his services; he was not to engage in the fur trade; and he was to offer his professional services free of charge to the company.

Samuel de Champlain had been quick to see that the terms were not sufficiently attractive to encourage immigrants. "The Companies having refused to give them the means of cultivating the land," he wrote,

had thus taken away all reason for them to become settlers. At the same time, these Companies gave out that there were numerous families in the country; the truth is that, being entirely useless, they served only to count, and burdened the settlement more than they helped it. . . . That was not the way to create a great desire on the part of anyone to go and people a country, when a man cannot have any free enjoyment of its returns. . . .

Men who knew the country best, like Father Le Jeune, could only agree with him. Those who emigrate for regular wages, he argued, do not provide the most efficient labor force; they "try to be like some of our neighbors, who, having scarcely passed the line of the Equator, all begin to call themselves Gentlemen, and no longer care to work; if they felt constrained to do it for themselves, they would not sleep over it." The right of ownership, even if limited, was his solution. He explained that immigrants ought to "engage themselves to some family for five or six years on the following conditions:"

That they should be boarded during all this time without receiving any wages, but also that they should possess entirely and in their own right one-half of all the land they clear. And, as they will need something for their own support, the contract should provide that all they get every year, from the lands they have already cleared, should be shared by half; this half, with the little profits they can make in the Country, would be enough to keep them, and to pay after the first or second year for half the tools which they will use in clearing and tilling the land. Now, if four men could clear eight arpents of land a year, doing nothing else, winter or summer, in six years forty-eight arpents would be cleared, of which twenty-four would belong to them. With these twenty-four arpents they could support thirty-six persons, or even forty-eight, if the land is good. Is this not a way of becoming rich in a little while?

Throughout the long history of New France, the concessions offered to immigrants assumed many different forms, but in the final analysis they amounted to the same thing—the promise, even the guarantee, of social mobility.

Those who came at their own expense had the promise of land and even, if they performed "notable service" in the interests of the authorities, of titles and patents of nobility. If, as now appears to be the case, most of the *engagés* did not have the promise of land at the time they agreed to their contracts of engagement, many did receive land after completion of their term of service; and, in any case, the wages they could expect in Canada allowed them a substantial increase in living standards.

To induce soldiers to remain in Canada after the period of their enlistment, land and financial subsidies were promised according to rank. Nearly 1500 remained, "finding there land that they would not perhaps have had in their own country." For skilled artisans there was not only the guarantee of high wages but, significantly, the promise that they would not forever be tied to the same position. Throughout the entire French occupation of Canada, ordinary craft restrictions on the achievement of mastership were loosened, and the opportunity to return to France in the higher status was freely granted. To be sure, the lure of the carrot was not the only means used; there was also the stick. Servants were forbidden to leave their masters and others to hide them on pain of severe punishment; marriage without consent of the master was banned; artisans were forced to do whatever their masters required, even when that meant working outside their trades; wages of unskilled workers were regulated.

The net effect of the administration's policy was to introduce slackness rather than rigidity into the society, even to the point of seriously compromising its own ability to obtain revenue. The state *corvée* had to be curtailed, eventually suppressed, for fear that word of its existence would restrict emigration from France and would antagonize the labor force, which, in another capacity, was counted on to provide militia service. The billeting of soldiers, always a source of complaint, was progressively limited until in 1683 it was entirely abolished and became a regular fixed charge upon the state. Direct payments in the form of seigniorial rents and ecclesiastical tithes were reduced considerably below the level prevailing in France. Indeed, *liberté* and *tranquilité*—eventually the major objectives of colonial policy—were seen as attainable only by offering concessions to induce a labor force to migrate and increase its productivity. "Such are the means of attracting colonists and keeping them," wrote M. Petit in his treatise on colonization. "But the most important of all is gentleness and moderation in the government, in extending its hand so that the colonists find, at least in the legitimate use of authority, compensations for the harshness of their labor and the sacrifice of their health in establishments recognized as so useful to the state."

Despite all inducements, the population of Canada never reached the desired quantity and quality. From beginning to end, the reports to the authorities bemoaned the scarcity of labor and its lack of discipline.

"Sixty indentured servants have been sent to this country again this year with the notion that they would be immediately useful," Intendant Jacques de Meulles wrote to the Marquis de Seignelay, Colbert's son, in 1684. "The oldest is not seventeen, and . . . I believe that those who sent them are making a mockery of us, there being no one of an age to render service." Send us no more gentlemen, Governor Denonville pleaded in 1686, only "sturdy peasants . . . used to hatchet and pickaxe." "We entreat you, Monseigneur," wrote Beauharnois and Hocquart to Minister Jean-Frédéric Phélypeaux, Marquis de Maurepas, in 1730, "to stop sending libertines to the colony. There is already a very great number, and it is more difficult to restrain them in this country than anywhere else because of the facility they have for escaping and the difficulty of convicting them." By 1712 the seigniory of Isle Perrot, granted in 1672, had only one inhabitant; those of Chicouanne and Boisseau, granted that same year, had none; Pointe du Lac, granted early in the seventeenth century, had one settler; Lussaudière, granted in 1672, had none; the seigniory of Jacques Cartier, granted in 1649, had only one inhabitant— he fished for eels—and dozens more were so sparsely inhabited as to be profitless to their owners and to the state. The problem of maintaining an adequate labor force was made even more difficult by the flight into the wilderness of those who were expected to remain fixed to the land. Throughout the eighteenth century, when the population of able-bodied adult males was always pathetically small, an average of three hundred men were absent each year, won over to the freedom of forest life, deserters to the English, or seekers after their fortune in Louisiana. Above all, however, the problem of disciplining labor and raising its productivity was exacerbated by the refusal of the population to behave in the expected manner. . . .

IV

The French government was faced with the twofold problem of maintaining order and stability in Canada and of motivating its subjects to perform the tasks given them. It sought to assign each man a status, the behavior of which was defined and regulated; when men behave according to prescription, each can act toward the other with the certainty that his own behavior will be understood and with the expectation that the other's responses will be the appropriate ones. At the same time, however, the government was faced with the necessity of recruiting a labor force, and the means it used involved offering such a variety of concessions and incentives that the position of the labor force in the society that was actually created was utterly different from its position in the society that had been contemplated. The government of France, like the General Court of the Virginia Company of London, was fully conscious of its problems, but—again like the Virginia Company—the solution it adopted for the problem of motivation made it impossible to solve the problem of order. Rigor and severe discipline, the distinguishing characteristics of the first social order in Canada as in Virginia, broke down in the face of the need to recruit a *voluntary* labor force. By her own actions, France created in Canada a social basis for disobedience, a society in which deviance became the only means of survival and of taking advantage of such opportunities as existed.

In a sense a drama was taking place on the North American continent that had been played out before in Europe. At various times in late medieval and early modern Europe, especially in periods of considerable stress, the seigniors had to offer concessions to their tenants, even to the point of enfranchisement, to prevent, by their emigration to "free" lands, the loss of their labor force. In 1439 the Hospitaliers de la Commanderie de Bure enfranchised their serfs of Thoisy: "all the 'houses and barns which are at the said Thoisy have been burned and destroyed . . . and no one wants to live . . . in the town. . . . in this way everyone withdraws and goes to live in free places.' " In 1628, when the Sire de Montureux-les-Gray, in Comte, freed his serfs, he did not conceal his hope that the "enfranchised village will be 'better inhabited and populated,' and, 'consequently,' that the seigniorial rights 'would produce greater revenue.' "

"Misery was sometimes the creator of liberty," says Marc Bloch.[3] So it undoubtedly was in Europe; in North America, the need to recruit a voluntary labor force was the mother of liberty.

---

[3] ED. NOTE: A modern authority on feudalism and feudal society.

English Colonial Society
in the Eighteenth Century

JACKSON TURNER MAIN

Jackson Turner Main, professor of history at the State University of New York, Stony Brook, represents a new breed of historians emphasizing quantifiable data in the reconstruction of the past. With a solid foundation in probate records, Professor Main has analyzed the social structure of the thirteen English colonies just prior to the American Revolution. He concludes that, whether tested by the existence of a class consciousness or by extreme economic stratification, English America was relatively classless. Although there was a rank order, one could move easily from one place in the order to another because of the open frontier and the lack of significant social or legal barriers to mobility. Canada, Diamond and McRae have both argued, had an open frontier, and although royal policy tried to set up barriers to movement westward (and upward in the social scale), the impediments were only partially successful. In Spanish America a vast, virtually limitless frontier offered itself to the white settlers, but law, custom, the economic and social systems, and the tendency to establish roots in metropolitan centers inhibited social mobility.

The juxtaposition of Main's essay with those of Leonard and Diamond shows the insights one can gain from comparative history. Essentially, Main contrasts pre-Revolutionary America with that which preceded and followed the epoch, casting strong doubts upon the arguments of those who emphasize class friction during the Revolutionary era. On the other hand, English America, he shows, had a permanent proletariat of Negro slaves, contrasted with New France which had none. For this reason, among others, society in the thirteen colonies, though far more mobile than that in Canada, contained even more divergent extremes in status. Furthermore, if we remember the position of the slave in the English colonies, we can more easily understand the creation of castes and a large Indian proletariat in Spanish America, where the colonizers had to come to grips with a large Indian population as well as with the Negroes they introduced as slaves. Finally, it might be argued,

From Jackson Turner Main, *The Social Structure of Revolutionary America*, Princeton University Press, 1965, pp. 270-286. Reprinted by permission of the Princeton University Press. Copyright © 1965 by The Princeton University Press.

using Main's essay as the basis, that the rigidity of Spanish colonial society enabled Spain to maintain her grip in the New World longer than did England with its relatively classless social structure. Does this suggest, too, that Louis XIV in his attempt to shape Canadian society along feudal lines, unwittingly glimpsed the future? Or—the reverse of the coin—could be British scheme have succeeded at all amidst a large native population? One last question also emerges: How did English colonial society of the seventeenth century compare with that in the eighteenth and with that of New France and Hispanic America in similar periods?

THE STUDENT OF REVOLUTIONARY SOCIETY MUST ASK TWO QUEStions: whether or not classes existed, and whether the social structure was democratic or undemocratic. If the word "class" requires the presence of class consciousness, if it can be used ónly when men are aware of a hierarchical structure and of their own rank within it, then this study indicates that America during the period 1763-1788 was relatively classless. Certainly it was both classless and democratic by comparison with the America of 1900 or with England in 1776. Moreover, rural New England, and the frontier and subsistence farming areas generally, furnish impressive evidence of a nearly equal division of wealth and a relative absence of classes.

If on the other hand the existence of classes does not depend upon class consciousness but implies nothing more than a rank order within which an individual can move up or down without any insurmountable difficulty, then revolutionary America can and indeed must be described in terms of classes. The society of the towns and of most commercial farm areas, the great distinctions between rich and poor, and the concentration of property, are decisive evidence of the presence of an economic class structure. Furthermore, a social hierarchy based upon a consciousness of class distinctions, a prestige order, can be identified, although it cannot be so precisely defined.

Although revolutionary America is seen to have contained classes, the question of democracy remains unsettled. On the one hand the societies in which class distinctions were prominent were aristocratic rather than equalitarian. In some commercial farm regions and in the major cities, a wealthy, fairly stable upper class had appeared, most of whose members had inherited their position, and who owned over half of the property; while a large lower class, often servile, also had developed. The opportunity to rise was restricted, or even denied altogether. In contrast the new country contained other sections in which most people were small property holders, wealth was equally distributed, and the poor man usually prospered. Revolutionary society was certainly not classless, yet neither was it entirely aristocratic. It contained the essential elements for an aristocracy while at the same time possessing the potential for a social and economic democracy.

There was, of course, a "permanent proletariat" consisting of those who always remained at the bottom. Slaves formed the largest part of this class. They totalled 23 percent of the whole population in 1760 and a little less than that thirty years later. Four-fifths of these were in the South, concentrated especially near the coast. A few sections of the country, then, contained a Negro labor force comprising considerably over half of the population, whereas most of the country had only a small such element, and vast areas none at all. Where slaves were scarce, white indentured servants or wageworkers were used instead. Less numerous than the Negroes, the white laborers usually formed only about one-fifth of the whites, though the proportion was doubled in certain areas. The exact number who remained in the lowest status is uncertain, but certainly fewer than half, possibly only one-fourth of them failed to become small property holders. Therefore out of twenty whites only one or two remained permanently poor. The evidence suggests that by the time of the Revolution even indentured servants had a chance of success nearly equal to that of the free workers. If this is true, then immigrants and native-born alike had reason to be confident about their future, and the few whites who failed were defeated not because of any external circumstance but because they lacked some essential quality. Thus the whole permanent proletariat, white and black, totalled less than 30 percent of the population.

At any point in time, revolutionary society contained a lower class comprising between one-third and two-fifths of the men. If defined by occupation, it included Negro slaves, white servants, and landless laborers employed by property owners such as farmers, artisans, and merchants. If defined by income, the lower class characteristically had almost none, except that they were given food, clothing, and shelter; free workers, however, did receive a money wage which enabled them to save. If defined by property, the men of this economic rank almost always had estates of less than £50, and usually they had none.

The free workers, with their money and opportunities for advancement, belonged to an intermediate category. They were partially independent, owned some property and perhaps some skill, were poor but not impoverished, and often were moving up into the middle class. Many farmers were no better off. There were, for example, numerous landowners in western Massachusetts and southern Delaware, the annual value of whose land was assessed at under £5; and according to the probate records (a more accurate indication of wealth) something like one-eighth of the yeomen had personal estates of less than £50. Many tenants were also poor, while perhaps 30 percent of the skilled artisans, especially many weavers, cordwainers, housewrights, coopers, and tailors, left very small estates. These men probably did earn enough to support their families adequately most of the time. Many of them moved from place to place, generally westward, perhaps improving their position, perhaps always balanced precariously upon the boundary between poverty and success. In England such men, together with the true lower class, constituted a latent threat to the existing order, and were kept under control by an educational system which (if it existed at all) taught them morality, by a religion which enjoined them to accept their lot submissively, and by force. In America, many members of this marginal class were young men with prospects. Discipline was rarely needed except by the slaves; even the uprisings of tenants and the flight of servants were not so much protests against their condition as a testimony to the opportunities which they knew existed.

The middle class in America consisted of small property holders who were usually self-employed. Its members are distinguished, at the lower end of the scale, from servants and slaves or others who had little or no property, and from the wage workers who depended entirely upon their daily labor; while at the other end they merge without any sharp definition into the upper class of men with large estates. Whereas the lower class lived at or barely above the subsistence level, the "middling sort" lived in comfort. The less fortunate among them usually owned at least £200 worth of real and personal property and netted perhaps £10 in excess of the minimum cost of living. The majority held property worth £400 to £500 and earned the £75 to £100 (or its equivalent) which supported their families in decency. The class included probably 70 percent of the whites and may be subdivided into the lower middle or marginal segment discussed above (roughly 20 percent), a middle middle (40 percent), and an upper middle (10 percent).

This largest and most important segment of revolutionary society was made up of several occupational groups. Small farmers were the most numerous element, comprising 40 percent of the whites and one-third of the whole population. If farmers who were substantial but not large landowners are added, the proportion rises to very nearly half of the whites and two-fifths of all the people. These farmers furnished most of their own necessities and earned at least £16 in cash (or credits) which permitted them to pay their debts and taxes, buy a few luxury articles, and save a little. Very few could hope to enlarge their farms without borrowing, but since they generally held 100 or 200 acres their prosperity depended more upon improving their methods and developing their land than upon adding acreage. Most of them could not provide for surplus sons, but the frontier or the towns took care of these. The more fortunate, who had good land in commercial farming areas, cleared much more than £16 and presented an agreeable picture of the ideal American, the prosperous farmer.

Second in number among the middling sort were the "artisans and mechanics" or "craftsmen." These were of two types. Some of them were not entrepreneurs but skilled workers who hired themselves out by the day, week, or year. Receiving from £40 to £50 annually, they could save a good deal of money so long as they remained single, but the married man just broke even; indeed if he had to rent a house and buy all of his food, £50 scarcely met expenses. Fortunately most of these artisans raised much of their own food and were thereby able to live in reasonable comfort and even acquire some property. Apparently almost half of them significantly improved their economic position.

The great majority of artisans in the rural areas, and probably a majority everywhere, were independent entrepreneurs who ordinarily kept a workshop in or near their houses. These were equivalent to farmers in that they were self-employed, but they usually ranked somewhat below the yeomen both in wealth and prestige. Their income and chance of increasing it depended upon their particular craft. The majority never rose above the middle rank, for the trades of cooper, cordwainer, blacksmith, tailor, weaver, or carpenter seldom provided a large return. On the other hand they also required little equipment and were in great demand, so that the apprentice could quite easily become a master. A few types of enterprise were by their nature more expensive to undertake and more profitable for the enterpriser. Distillers, ropemakers, goldsmiths, and the like were capitalists whose economic position compared favorably with that of prosperous farmers and many professional men.

Professional men as a whole also belonged to the middle class, earning considerably more than most farmers and artisans but not enough to raise them decisively into the economic elite. Two segments of the professional group were exceptional. Lawyers ordinarily received large incomes and formed part of the "better sort," while teachers often had so little property that they ranked economically even below skilled workers, though they may have had greater prestige. The other professionals, among whom ministers and doctors were the most numerous, typically earned £100 to £200, a sum which allowed some luxuries and enabled them to accumulate £500 worth of property. This property in turn added to their income and further raised their standard of living. They therefore could spare the cash to educate their children for the professions or for trade: indeed it seems possible that the clergy at least was to a large extent a self-recruiting group, partly because most Americans could not send their children to school whereas the ministers could and did. In the middle class too belonged the overseers, innkeepers, ships' captains, retailers, clerks, and most government officials.

The upper class was composed of large property owners. By European standards there was, of course, no upper class at all, since there was no hereditary aristocracy. There were in certain areas families who had retained wealth and position for several generations, and who were then and have been since called "aristocrats"; but the word, if it is to be used at all, must be defined to fit the American scene. Probably it is better simply to structure revolutionary society on its own terms. Entrance into the upper class followed at once upon election to certain public offices, and most often upon acquiring a certain amount of property. Any definition is certainly arbitrary, but a reasonable one is the ownership of £2,000, which made one well-to-do, or of £5,000, which meant wealth. The southern planter who owned 500 acres and 20 slaves possessed at least the former sum, which was, incidentally, the amount required for membership in the South Carolina Senate. Probably 10 percent of the landowners, the same proportion of ministers and doctors, most lawyers, a few artisans, and not far from half of the merchants qualified as well-to-do or wealthy—the total being roughly 10 percent of the whites. These men had incomes which were almost by definition in excess of £500,[1] and they controlled about 45 percent of the country's wealth.[2] It is important to remember that this was not a closed class. Another tenth of the men owned estates of £1,000 or so, and movement from one rank

[1] Not all of this £500 had to be in cash, of course. Most well-to-do farmers probably cleared far less than this, but supplied much of their own food, fuel, and shelter.

[2] Anyone who uses this figure for comparing the distribution of wealth then and now should be informed that the slaves are not here included as part of the population. If they are added, the figure becomes a little higher because the population is larger by nearly one-fourth, so that more individuals would be included among the top tenth of property holders. Their share of the wealth would become about 50 percent over-all. The following table shows the appropriate situation. Figures in parentheses are obtained when slaves are included.

Share of Wealth of the Richest 10%

	North	South
Frontier	33%	40% (40+)
Subsistence farm	35	40 (45)
Commercial farm	45-50	55 (65)
City	55-60	60+ (65)
General	45	50 (55)

to another was frequent. Although the very wealthiest Virginia planters formed a fairly tight social group, it is probable that entrance into the lesser planter society was much easier. The urban elite even before the Revolution contained many men who began life with little property.

Such was the class structure of the United States viewed as a whole. There were, however, several quite different sub-societies based upon geographical and historical factors. Each colony had in 1763 certain peculiarities, and the contrast between North Carolina and Virginia, adjacent though they were, was as striking as that between the Old Dominion and New Hampshire. Moreover every colony contained three or four distinct social structures. Fortunately these sub-societies reappear everywhere so that the country can still be treated as a whole.

Most colonies still had a frontier area. Pioneer societies were of two types. In some cases land speculators obtained large tracts which they then rented, sold, or occasionally farmed. Ordinarily the speculator was not a resident, so that no upper class was present, but real property was more than usually concentrated in the hands of large proprietors, while the lower class of landless men was more numerous than on most frontiers. The typical frontier class structure, however, was "democratic": most men belonged to the middle class, property was equally distributed, and the poor man found it easy to become a farmer.

Subsistence—or more accurately subsistence-plus—farms existed wherever the farmers could raise or market little produce in excess of their immediate needs. Poor soil, inadequate transportation, lack of capital, or a shortage of labor, were inhibiting factors. Since agriculture was not particularly profitable under these circumstances, few wealthy men lived in such areas. The lower class also was small, for few men could afford servants or slaves, while the hired hand quickly obtained a farm of his own or left for better soils. The great majority of the men were small farmers who, together with a few artisans and professional men, formed a very large middle class. Property was equally distributed; the subsistence farm society, like that of the frontier, was democratic.

In areas where agriculture was profitable, commercial farming developed. The result might be only a general increase in the prosperity of small farmers, but typically some landowners became rich, controlled an increasing amount of the property, and bought or hired an expanding labor force. Class distinctions quickly appeared. The society (at least in the North) also became more diversified because the large farmers tended to specialize in staple crops and to buy whatever else they needed, while their higher incomes allowed them to purchase luxuries. More artisans were present, more traders, and more professional men. The southern "plantation" social structure did not ordinarily contain such a large non-farm element (unless some slaves are counted as artisans), but exceeded the northern commercial farm sections in the size of the upper and lower classes, the concentration of property, and the general wealth. While the commercial farm area was first undergoing development, men were able quickly and easily to increase their property and prestige. Once that process had been completed, opportunities for those without capital diminished and class lines tended to harden.

By contrast, urban societies everywhere offered opportunity to men of all ranks. The cities contained many wage earners and some slaves, so that the lower class was even larger than in commercial farm regions, except for those parts of the South in which slaves were especially numerous. With the same exception the towns contained the highest proportion of wealthy men, who had an unusually large share of the city's property. Despite the economic inequalities which characterized urban society, the middle class was seldom less than half of the whole population, the general standard of living was high, and economic opportunities in a great variety of occupations afforded the poor man a chance to acquire property.

Just as the unequal distribution of property proves the existence of economic classes, so also the different styles of living testify to the inequality of income. The revolutionary family which had to pay cash for everything needed at least £50 annually. The lower class and even some skilled workers received less than this. Had they depended entirely upon a cash income, they must have lived below the subsistence level, but fortunately several factors intervened to save almost all of these people from actual want. The majority—slaves and indentured servants —were supported by their masters. Others owned a little land on which they produced much of their food. Still others were single men without dependents who needed much less money and in fact could save a little. By the time they married they usually had acquired a farm or a skill which raised them into the middle class. Therefore the members of the lower class were guaranteed at least an adequate livelihood.

The middle class generally enjoyed a comfortable living. Small farmers did without much money but raised almost all of their food, made some of their clothing, and supplied other household needs, so that they usually showed a net cash profit. Professional men, substantial farmers and artisans, and other members of what was by colonial standards an upper middle class, generally exceeded the £100 or thereabouts which their style of living required. The upper class too was fortunate. Merchants, lawyers, and planters very seldom earned enough to live like European aristocrats, but in the new world £400 or so would enable anyone who produced his own food to live like a gentleman.

Crucially important to the early American was his ability to improve his economic and social position. Comparisons with other societies are dangerous when there are no comparable facts, but the evidence points decisively toward a much higher degree of mobility in revolutionary America than had been usual elsewhere. Several circumstances contributed to this result. One was of course the absence for most Americans of legal or social impediments. All whites were permitted to acquire property, and as they did so they progressed up the social scale, acceptance even at the higher levels coming almost at once. Another factor was the general economic expansion combined with a rapid growth in the population. There was always more room at the top. Important too were the vast quantities of unoccupied land, some of it excellent, available at a low price with several years to pay. This land contained untouched natural resources, notably lumber. Finally, the American could move easily from place to place. Had he been in some manner constrained within his home neighborhood, his prospects would have been considerably diminished, for economic opportunities in the older farm areas, while greater than in Europe, were much less than in the newer regions; but he was always able to move to the town or to the frontier

This geographical mobility did not usually involve long-distance migration. The occupation of western Pennsylvania, Kentucky, and Tennessee naturally required a considerable journey, but during the years 1763-1788 most of the movement was local, the distance travelled short. The young man moved a few score miles at most, to a town or country lying roughly westward as transportation facilities dictated. The occupation of a frontier, as far as the present study reveals the situation, was carried out by those living adjacent to it. The westward course seldom was reversed: for few men returned to the east. Probably the process was largely a rural phenomenon, for city folk did not have the farmer's skills, and ordinarily stayed in the towns. There may have been some movement of artisans to the country where they continued to practice their trades, but opportunities in the towns (at least in the North) were good enough so that a "safety valve" was seldom needed.

The man who started without property had the best chance of advancement if he went west. Indeed four out of five pioneers obtained land, usually within a few years after their arrival. Immigrants, even indentured servants, had nearly as good a chance for success as native-born whites; the failures occurred among the unskilled regardless of their origin. Those frontier areas subject to large-scale speculation sometimes offered less opportunity to the prospective landowners—much of the land in New York and northern Virginia was rented to tenants rather than sold—but ordinarily the man with some skill was almost certain of entering the middle class.

If he lived in an older community the certainty was gone but the probability of advancement was still fairly high. About one out of three landless laborers in such areas obtained land without moving out of the county. More than half of the artisans advanced economically and even indentured servants had some success. Obviously the fact that the good land had long since been occupied was the principal limiting factor, and had all of the people stayed put, those at the bottom might have been fated to remain there. Fortunately the constant movement out of the country created openings locally, and if one failed to seize the chance, there was always another one farther west.

But though someone of ability might look forward with confidence to entering the rural middle class, he could seldom achieve higher rank. If the situation in Virginia is at all typical, an established rural upper class admitted very few new members. Those who made good came not from among the small farmers but from the businessmen and lawyers. Admittedly conclusions based upon one colony ought not to be pushed too far, but it seems that in the South it was rare for any parvenu to achieve eminence among the landholders (by revolutionary times) unless he did so through buying land on a frontier which rapidly became commercial. Probably the same was true in the North.

Urban society was much more open than that of the commercial farm areas. Although the unskilled workers (including mariners) seldom acquired much property, the chance of becoming an independent artisan was excellent in those occupations which demanded little venture capital. Success in the larger enterprises and in commerce was more difficult. Nevertheless even the wealthy merchant class of colonial New York was composed partly of self-made men: whereas not over one in ten wealthy Virginians were *nouveaux riches,* about one in three members of the Chamber of Commerce were of humble origin. The proportion of self-made men was even higher after the war, but this probably was an abnormal situation due to the forcible displacement of Loyalist merchants by enterprising rebels.

Just as the revolutionary American could increase his wealth, he could also advance in prestige. The "social class" or "status" order which the colonists brought with them from Europe was based upon a hereditary system of ranks, symbolized or identified by the discriminatory use of titles. This hierarchical society (which even in England was not inflexible) gradually disappeared in America partly because no European aristocracy was present to perpetuate it, but largely because of the actual condition of social equality and the remarkable ease with which the colonial could improve his position. Therefore the old order was eventually replaced by one which developed out of the new economic circumstances. The indigenous class structure was based upon property rather than inherited status.[3] When a new prestige order was created, it corresponded closely with economic classes. It seems reasonable to suppose that, since titles-were losing their symbolic significance, the Americans found a substitute in their style of life, by which they distinguished themselves visibly from their inferiors.

The outcome made social advancement relatively easy. Perhaps the principal method was simply by making money, for there were no social barriers which property could not surmount, and there existed a general admiration for the man who acquired an estate. A high regard for material possessions permitted anyone to achieve status approximately in proportion to his income. Another way of winning esteem was to obtain a high political office. The degree of democracy during the revolutionary era is disputed, but no one denies that preferment included Americans from more walks of life than was the case with contemporary European officialdom; while the Revolution itself unquestionably opened the doors to a greater number of artisans and farmers. The position of justice of the peace did not mean quite so much as in England but it was still an important and prestigeful office which could be reached, at least in the North, by men of small property. Education, though available principally to the upper class, occasionally elevated the man of merit, while during the war some soldiers of lowly birth won high rank and universal regard.

This social mobility was of course limited just as was economic mobility. Titles still had some significance. The great majority of "esquires" were large property holders, while "gentlemen" owned about twice the average wealth. Still, only a minority of the upper class merited the "esquire," while in the North most of the "gentlemen" and one-third of the "esquires" were of humble birth, and "Mr." meant practically nothing at all anywhere. Despite the frequent public eulogies addressed to farmers, they had no monopoly of these symbols of prestige, for such titles were granted to merchants, professional men, and even to artisans.

Although Americans seemed to express an excessive regard for farmers and were publicly critical of lawyers and traders, they had a generally accurate view of their own society. They preferred to think of it as one of equality and proudly pointed to such features as the large middle

[3] See Sigmund Diamond, *The Creation of Society in the New World* (Chicago, 1963); Bernard Bailyn, "Politics and Social Structure in Virginia," in James Morton Smith, ed., *Seventeenth-Century America: Essays in Colonial History* (Chapel Hill, 1959), 90-115.

class, the absence of beggars, the comfortable circumstances of most people, and the limitless opportunities for those who worked hard and saved their money. Still, few had any illusion that perfection had been achieved. The existence of slaves and poor whites, of rich merchants and planters, and of what seemed to many an increasing concentration of wealth, prevented any complacency and aroused anxious criticism of the inequalities which marred the vision of the Good Society. Our modern division of American society into three classes corresponds closely to their contemporary analysis, and they likewise recognized the economic basis of class. European travellers similarly saw that the American social structure, while far less aristocratic and more fluid than that of the Old World, had obvious economic and social inequalities.

Cultural distinctions were even more evident. Just as the prestige order paralleled the economic class structure, so did the culture reflect one's wealth.[4] The much higher incomes of the "better sort" made possible a standard of living which visibly distinguished them from the rest of the people. These differences existed not only in their food and drink, their use of silver, and their clothing, but in the architectural style of their homes, the paintings adorning the walls of their houses, and the music they enjoyed. Attendance at the theater was principally an upper-class activity. The possession of books varied with one's income. Most of the lower sort had none. Members of the middle class did own books, but usually they had only a few, which were almost entirely religious in nature. On the other hand almost all of the wealthy men—especially if they were professionals—had libraries which often included a great variety of works. The ordinary American was also deprived of the education which might have raised his income, his status, and his cultural level. Slaves almost never learned to write; servants rarely did so; and wage-workers seldom exceeded a bare literacy. Even members of the middle class were seriously handicapped. Only in New England were free schools available, and private institutions were rare on the frontier or in subsistence farm areas. The tuition charged by private schools was low enough so that children of middle-class families could attend, but only if they lived at home. The cost of room and board prevented all but the larger property holders from sending their sons away. Therefore few farmers or artisans could hope for a higher education. The possibility did exist, however, especially in the northeast and above all in New England, which thereby came closer than any other section to achieving the American ideal of equal opportunity.

[4] An excellent description of colonial culture from this point of view is contained in Max Savelle, *Seeds of Liberty* (New York, 1948).

INDIAN POLICY IN COLONIAL AMERICA

Spanish Indian Policy in Colonial America: The Ordering of Society

J. H. PARRY

Obviously, the Indian populace played a major role in the Spanish empire, but except as trading partners and as allies or enemies in colonial wars, the natives played only a minor part in the English and French empires. Spain had to deal with many sedentary, semicivilized groups of Indians with well-

From J. H. Parry, *The Spanish Seaborne Empire,* London and New York, 1966, pp. 173-191. Reprinted by permission of Hutchinson Publishing Group Ltd. and Alfred A. Knopf, Inc. Copyright © 1966 by J. H. Parry.

developed institutions; in North America, England and France confronted tribes far more backward, predominantly hunters but good enough farmers to teach some techniques to the newcomers. Even if one ignores, for the moment, the sharp distinctions in the backgrounds of the three colonial powers, it was still virtually inevitable that Spanish policy toward the Indians should differ sharply from that of England and France.

In the first selection in this section, J. H. Parry, Gardiner Professor of Oceanic History and Affairs at Harvard University, discusses the methods used to fit the Indian into Spain's New World society. His treatment begins with the years just after the discovery of America and moves forward to the eve of the epoch described by Irving Leonard. Parry's principal theme is the conflict between the humanitarian conscience of the lawgivers and the practical realities of colonial life.

Reading this selection, one is struck by the incongruities, self-deceptions, rationalizations, and medieval character of Spanish policy. The idea that freedom and permanent compulsory labor, no matter how well regulated in theory, are compatible is a concept difficult to grasp, even if one finds it no more inhumane than the British policy of driving the Indians from their homes into the hinterland. The whole idea of *indios capaces* is difficult for twentieth-century man to reconcile, given even the refractory personalities and policies of the early conquistadores. One wonders, too, to what degree the waverings and inconsistencies of Spanish monarchs and their advisers and their repeated capitulations to colonial realities were owing to tactical considerations, and to what degree to a lack of deep concern for the welfare of the Indians. For the student of comparative colonial systems, Parry's discussion poses a fundamental question: Would France and England have responded in a similar way in the same circumstances at the same point in time?

T HE SPANISH COMMUNITY IN THE NEW WORLD INCLUDED NO PEAS-ants and virtually no manual labourers. In all pre-industrial societies a community dominated by a military caste tends to discount the social and ethical value of manual labour, and New World Spaniards displayed this prejudice in an extreme form. Their numbers included settlers —*encomenderos* and their followers, ranchers, mine-owners—a class of armed subjects of great privilege and in some instances, within a generation of settlement, of considerable wealth; a clergy numerous in relation to the total number of Spaniards, but mere drops in the ocean of the Indian population; a considerable and rapidly increasing body of officials, lawyers, notaries and miscellaneous quill-drivers; a few merchants, shopkeepers and craftsmen, mostly in the few big towns. The new Spanish economy in the Indies depended on the old Indian economy for much of its food—particularly grain, vegetables, and poultry, all mainly produced by Indians—and for almost all its labour; for except in the islands and a few places on the Caribbean coast, the import of African slaves was too small to be of major significance. Without Indian labour the Spanish community could not exist. Most Indians, however, accustomed to a life of communal subsistence farming, would not willingly work for outside employers; and the Indians, by reason of their standing as Christian neophytes, by reason of their relatively defenceless condition, and in virtue of repeated royal declarations, had a special claim upon the crown for protection. The agents of royal paternalism were expected to defend the personal liberty of the Indians, without denying the just claims of deserving conquerors and settlers; to ensure an adequate supply of labour for the Spanish settlements, while protecting the Indians in their possession of land, which relieved them of the necessity of working for wages; above all, to safeguard and increase the revenue which the crown derived from the Indies and on which, throughout the sixteenth century, it came more and more to depend. Clearly these objects of royal policy conflicted. The crown received annually hundreds of petitions from individuals or groups, seeking favours which, in many instances, could be granted at the expense of someone else's interests. The answers to them could be yes or no; but in giving any answers the crown, the fount of justice, implied general guiding principles of social organization. Dozens of reports, complaints and recommendations from clergy, officials and municipal corporations, arrived with every fleet, suggesting from every conceivable point of view what those principles ought to be. The crown endeavoured to select and decide, and to make its decisions explicit, in a steady stream of legislation. Nothing in the story of the Indies is more impressive than this immense body of statute law, which in 1680 was collected, roughly collated and published as the *Recopilación de los leyes de las Indias*. Many decrees concerned immediate matters of detail, and consistency in them is hard to find. From time to time, however, the crown issued general legislative enactments for the Indies as a whole. These general decrees or codes were serious and conscientious attempts to reconcile conflicting interests. It is possible to trace in them—though with many vacillations and inconsistencies—the development of conscious official policy in the ordering of colonial society.

Almost every Spanish enactment concerning the treatment of the Indians insisted that they were free men. There were slaves in the Indies, of course, not only Africans imported as slaves but Indians who had been captured in the act of rebellion and enslaved as a punishment; but these latter were exceptions. The normal status of an Indian under Spanish rule was held to be that of legal liberty, and it is essential to an understanding of Spanish legislation to appreciate what 'liberty' meant in this context. It meant freedom to move about, to change one's place of residence at will; to own property (subject at times to certain exceptions such as horses and fire-arms, for reasons both of security and of social 'degree'); freedom to sue and to be sued (subject to rules defining the different value placed upon the testimony of different classes of people) and unrestricted access to the appropriate courts; freedom to choose an occupation, to change one's occupation and one's employer. It certainly did not mean freedom to hold and practise false religion, once the true religion had been revealed (though the bishops treated Indians far more leniently in this respect than they did Spaniards, and the Holy Office in the sixteenth century had no jurisdiction over them). Nor—and this was the crucial point—did liberty mean freedom to be idle, to be left to one's own devices, to refrain from making any contribution to the well-being of society and the revenue of the crown. The King protected his subjects, did justice among them, upheld their rights, according to their respective stations. In return, the feudatory, the *encomendero*, was expected to bear arms; the cleric to preach and pray; the peasant, the Indian villager, to work and to support the others by his work. In short, the liberty of the Indian, in the sense in which Spanish legislators used the word, meant, *mutatis mutandis,* the kind of liberty which a legally free peasant enjoyed in Spain; liberty within the context of the whole society to which he belonged, and subject to discharging the appropriate obligations towards that society, as laid down by custom.

Within a very few years of the first settlement in Hispaniola the crown was made aware, by the settlers' complaints and petitions, of the difficulty of applying Spanish notions of social order to a people who habitually lived in 'idleness'; who lived, that is to say, by a primitive, hand-to-mouth subsistence agriculture supplemented by hunting and fishing. In these circumstances, compulsion, in order to make the natives do a reasonable amount of work in the public interest, was not thought incompatible with their free status. Compulsory labour of one kind or another was common in Europe, and those of whom it was required were not confused with slaves. The instructions given to Ovando[1] as governor illustrate this point. On his appointment he was told to proclaim to the Indians that they were free men, and might move about the island as they wished. They were to pay tribute only as all the King's subjects did; they could be compelled to work only on royal service, either in the gold washing or on public works; no Spaniard was to rob or harm them. Within a few months of his arrival Ovando reported that the

[1] ED. NOTE: Nicolás de Ovando, early governor of Hispaniola, who sailed there from Spain in 1502 with over 2,500 persons to put the settlement on a permanent basis. He governed for six years.

Indians, on being told they were free men, ran off into the bush and left the settlements without food or labour. His powers of compulsion, accordingly, were strengthened in a fresh series of instructions sent to him in 1503: the Indians were to be made to settle in organised villages; each village was to be placed under the protection of a Spanish patron, who was to provide a school and a priest; for convenience of employment, the villages were to be sited near the 'mines'—that is, near to gold-bearing streams; Indians could be ordered to work, when necessary, not only in 'mines' but in building and cultivation, and not only for the crown but for private employers; periods of employment were to be moderate and wages reasonable; in addition to his employment, each Indian was to have a house and a plot of land, which he might not alienate; intermarriage between Spaniards and Indians was to be encouraged; and in all things Indians were to be treated 'as free men, for such they are.'

These instructions, needless to say, were completely at variance with Taino custom and quite beyond the power of a rudimentary colonial government to enforce. Ovando interpreted them as permission to extend the tentative *repartimiento* of Columbus's day: to divide up the entire male population of Hispaniola in lots of roughly 100 or multiples of 100, under the name and legal form (with which, as a *comendador* of Alcántara, he must have been familiar in Spain) of *encomienda*. Each group of Indians was assigned to a Spaniard who—subject to the obligations and limits set out in the instructions—might employ their services as he chose. To the *encomienda* in this crude and early form Ferdinand, as regent of Castile, gave legislative approval in a decree of 1509, which provided that on completion of any new conquest, the *adelantado* or governor might divide up the natives of the area among the conquerors.

The *encomienda* of Ovando's day infringed the legal liberty of the Indians, in that instead of laying on them a general compulsion to work (which was held to be compatible with liberty) it placed them in permanent *personal* servitude to individual Spaniards. It was open to grave objection, therefore, on grounds of principle. More obvious and immediate, however, was the human suffering which could be caused by such unlimited—because unsupervised—subjection. The Spanish settlers were themselves suffering severe hardships. Many died shortly after arrival. The energies of the survivors were concentrated primarily upon an eager search for gold; but they had also to keep alive, to find food, to build themselves habitable dwellings. Between their excited gold-fever and their fierce struggle to survive there was no room in their minds for sympathy or sense of responsibility. They could feel only a furious irritation towards impractical, unreliable savages, who had no notion of steady work, who were for ever running off into the woods, or else unpredictably dying. The Indians were indeed dying in great numbers; so their masters, to maintain the production of gold, drove and flogged the survivors in order to get the last ounce of work out of them before they died too. These were the crimes which horrified the Dominican missionaries, fresh from Spain, who arrived in Hispaniola in 1510. Of the many causes of Indian depopulation, some—social disruption, infanticide, despair—were incomprehensible to Europeans; others—starvation and pestilence—were acts of God, the familiar, unavoidable lot of many in Spain and everywhere. The missionaries had little to say about these. Their indignation was reserved for the horrors which they thought preventable: the flogging, the slave-driving and the institution of the *encomienda* which permitted them.

The first open attack on the system by a Spaniard was made in 1511, in a series of indignant sermons preached at Santo Domingo by the Dominican Antonio de Montesinos, and followed by the refusal of communion to some *encomenderos*. The sermons created a great stir in Hispaniola, and, when reported, gave serious offense in official circles in Spain. The viceroy, Diego Colón, was told to put a stop to further public discussion of the subject by missionaries. Montesinos made a hurried journey to Spain in the hope of convincing the King's advisers of the seriousness of the situation. In this he apparently succeeded; as was customary in matters of public controversy of this sort, the Crown appointed a committee, whose members included both ecclesiastics and officials, to examine the allegations which had been made and to propose plans for reform. The result of their deliberations was the promulgation, late in 1512, of the Laws of Burgos, the first general code governing the status and treatment of the natives in the Spanish Indies. The *encomiendas* and the forced labour system in general were retained, except that the right to 'commend' Indians (which had been withheld from the viceroy in 1511) was now explicitly reserved to the Crown. Every male Indian was required to spend nine months of the year in Spanish employment, and one-third of the total labour force was to be employed in gold production. On the other hand, while legalising forced labour, the legislators endeavoured to limit its abuses. The code contained emphatic and detailed regulations prescribing the hours of work, the housing, clothing, feeding and instruction of Indian workers. Except in their codified detail these two sections of the Laws contained little innovation; the first was a concession to a colonial economic necessity and to the need for revenue, the second a concession to conscience and to humanitarian pressure. The principal innovation in the code concerned the concept of

Indian liberty. The legislators accepted the liberty of the Indians in principle, but decided that most Indians were in practice incapable of making use of their liberty. A distinction was drawn between those who were *capaces* and those, the majority, who were not; the *capaces* being Indians who were able and willing to embrace Christianity and adopt a European manner of life, and who, within limits, could be trusted to govern themselves These *Indios capaces* were to be 'set free' free, presumably, from the *encomienda* system, since, being civilised, they would accept voluntarily the necessity of regular wage-earning employment. They were to be gathered in villages under their own headmen, subject to supervision by Spanish priests and officials. The *encomenderos* who lost their services were to be compensated from the tribute revenue. In order to increase the numbers of *Indios capaces,* intelligent Indians were to be selected for training as teachers, and the sons of chiefs were to be taught—among other things—Latin.

The Laws of Burgos, with their curious mixture of naïveté and cynicism, naturally proved a bitter disappointment to the Dominican pressure group, and attempts to enforce them—in so far as any attempts were made—were more disappointing still. In 1514 commissioners were sent out to revise the distribution of Indians on behalf of the Crown, but the only result of their activities was the suppression of some of the settlers' grants and the transfer of large numbers of Indians to absentee *encomenderos,* chiefly the royal secretary Conchillos and his Aragonese friends about the court, who employed colonial agents to keep their Indians at work washing for gold. The death of Ferdinand, however, the regency of Jiménez and the eclipse of Fonseca and Conchillos, brought a change of attitude at court. The mantle of Montesinos had fallen upon the formidable Las Casas, who in 1516 succeeded in enlisting the sympathy of the regent. Diego Colón was absent from his government and absorbed in litigation in Spain over his hereditary rights. Jiménez seized the opportunity to send out to Hispaniola a commission of three Jeronymite friars, to take over the government, to enforce the Laws of Burgos, in particular the clauses for the protection of Indians, and to report on the whole problem of native policy. The arrival of the triumvirate at the end of 1516 caused general alarm among the settlers, but little came of their mission. They cancelled the *encomiendas* which had been granted to absentees, but their conscientious efforts to gather 'capable' Indians in free villages were all failures; the Indians ran away as before. In their reports the Jeronymites confirmed that the colony could not survive without forced labour. Their principal positive recommendations concerned the emigration of Spanish farmers, to be encouraged by grants of seed and tools; and—with many misgivings—the import into the Indies of Negro slaves to relieve part of the burden of labour borne by the Indians. Spanish planters—many of them from the Canaries—and Negro slaves were in fact soon to form the chief elements in the Antillean population, as the Indians died out. In 1520 Diego Colón, having succeeded in some, but not all, of his claims, resumed his government. Las Casas, bitterly disappointed in Hispaniola, had gone back to Spain, and in 1521 embarked on a social experiment of his own: the settlement upon the Venezuela coast, of a community of Spanish farmers and artisans living a common Christian life under priestly direction, supporting themselves by their own efforts without recourse to forced labour. The object of the enterprise was conversion by force of example. It failed as completely as the free villages of Hispaniola; the settlers were massacred by the local Indians. Even Las Casas' spirit was crushed, for a time, by this disaster. He took the Dominican habit and retired to a monastery in Santo Domingo, where he lived, in seclusion for the next eight years.

Between the disillusion of Hispaniola and the catastrophe of Cumaná, however, Las Casas and other Dominicans about the court had achieved one important success. They had gained the ear of the young King Charles, and implanted in the King's mind a lasting disapproval of the *encomienda* system, with its feudal implications and its opportunities for abuse. This deep suspicion and dislike, shared by many of Charles's advisers, influenced official native policy throughout his reign. Among the many causes of Indian suffering, the *encomienda* was singled out—wrongly—as the principal, the most serious, grievance. The Council of the Indies were soon made aware of the unique efficacy of the *encomienda* as an instrument of settlement, but they thought of it as—at best—a temporary makeshift, to be abandoned and replaced by a purely official administration when the settlements were secure. Over and over again they made legislative or administrative attacks on the institution. The attacks were met by sulky non-compliance on the part of officials; by strident protests from *encomenderos;* by gloomy predictions of abandonment of settlements, of loss of revenue, of general chaos and disaster; sometimes by armed revolt. Alarmed by these demonstrations, the Council would retreat, restore some of the *encomenderos'* privileges, equivocate over others, sometimes even make further concessions. At the same time the royal conscience would be salved by more and more stringent rules against abuses. These repeated short-term vacillations of royal policy are confusing to the historian, and were extremely unsettling for the colonists; but the general tendency throughout the reign was consistent—to define the rights of *encomenderos* over their Indians in more and more restrictive terms. In the process the institution, though not formally abolished—government was not strong enough for that—became much modified, and lost much of its original importance. It was supplemented, however, and eventually largely replaced, by other systems of exploitation, economically more efficient but socially no less oppressive.

The *encomiendas* of New Spain, established as they were among numerous, vigorous and settled peoples, were far more remunerative and far less oppressive than those of the islands; but they were no less repugnant to Charles and his councillors. The suspicion with which Cortés was regarded at court throughout his active life arose in large measure from his action in granting *encomiendas* in New Spain without prior authority. In 1523 he was ordered to revoke his grants, and to make no more. He appealed against the order and postponed its enforcement, explaining—truthfully—that without *encomiendas* the conquest could not be held. His explanation was borne out by a series of indignant petitions from his followers. In a series of general ordinances issued from Granada in 1526, and elaborated in 1528 and 1529, the government reluctantly gave way: if it was thought necessary for their conversion, Indians might be distributed in *encomiendas* 'as free persons.' They were not to be robbed, ill-treated or hired out to third parties; the tribute exacted from them must be reasonable, and their labour must be paid. Commended Indians might not be employed in mining or made to carry burdens. Before the conquest almost all land transport had been on men's backs; but Spanish officials and clerics unaccustomed to this practice were shocked by the spectacle of trotting *tamemes,* balancing their immense shoulder-loads on tumplines over their heads, much as modern Europeans are shocked to see coolies pulling rickshaws. They disliked the affront to human dignity; and they knew the solution. Just as rickshaws today can be towed by bicycles, so Indian porters could, in time, be replaced by mules. As for mining, it could be done by slaves, whether captured in rebellion, purchased from Indian chiefs or imported from abroad. Such arduous work was not for 'free persons.'

The exchanges of 1523-9 well illustrate the uncertainties of a colony which could not be sure, from one year to the next, of its labour supply. Wage-earning employment was, to the Indians, unfamiliar and initially unattractive. The *encomienda* was the only lawful device whereby individual settlers could exert pressure in order to secure the labour they needed for building a society of European type. The Crown might—at least in theory—abolish the whole system at any time by a stroke of the pen. Even while the *encomienda* was upheld in law, the control of labour which it conferred was too brief and impermanent to be satisfactory to the settlers. The duration of *encomienda* grants had never been clearly decided. Some of the island assignments had been for periods as brief as three years; and the determination of settlers to make the most of them while they lasted had been the cause of much heartless brutality. No time limit was set in the grants by Cortés; they were generally assumed to be for life, and it would have been extremely difficult in practice to dispossess the recipients while they lived. *Encomenderos* repeatedly pressed for legislation making their grants hereditary and perpetual, like the *mayorazgos,* the entailed estates, which had been legalised in Spain by the Laws of Toro and which were rapidly gaining popularity among property owners there. Cortés, in his despatches, pleaded for perpetual *encomiendas:* so, curiously, did Zumárraga, who was officially protector of Indians for New Spain as well as Bishop of Mexico. Both argued plausibly that perpetuity would be a guarantee of social stability and economic development, and would encourage among *encomenderos* a sense of paternal responsibility for their Indians. These arguments were resisted, naturally, by Spanish settlers who had no *encomiendas* and hoped that their turn would come, and by the Crown, which wished to retain its control over the granting of *encomiendas* even if it could not, in practice, abolish them.

When the *audiencia*[2] of New Spain was established in 1528 the instructions to its members included a census of Indians, to serve as the basis for a redistribution of *encomiendas,* which might then be made hereditary. The task was beyond the resources of the colonial administration; and Nuño de Guzmán and his colleagues were too busy feathering their own nests, creating *encomiendas* for themselves and prosecuting their vendetta against Cortés, even to attempt it. By the time of their dismissal and replacement by a new Bench in 1530, policy had changed again, largely as a result of Zumárraga's reports of the brutalities which Nuño had permitted. Another royal committee, sitting at Barcelona, had reconsidered the whole question of *encomiendas* and had pronounced against them. The second *audiencia,* accordingly, was instructed in 1530 —though the instruction was not made public—to arrange for the resumption of *encomiendas* by the Crown, beginning with new grants recently made by Nuño de Guzmán, with a view to the gradual elimination of the institution. Crown Indians, and ultimately all Indians, were to be placed in the administrative care of district officers, *corregidores*—the first mention, in legislation on native affairs, of this important official. Slave-raiding in the frontier districts, and the deliberate provocation of rebellion in order to justify enslavement, were to be stopped.

The new *oidores* made tentative moves to carry out their instructions,

[2] ED. NOTE: A combination colonial court of appeals and advisory council for viceroys and governors.

which naturally provoked opposition and protest; so, like most colonial officials, they came eventually to the conclusion that the task was hopeless, and the project was again dropped. The instructions issued to Antonio de Mendoza, who went out to New Spain in 1535 as the first viceroy, marked a return of the *encomienda* to royal favour; and general legislation of that year made a further important concession: *encomiendas* might, on the death of their holders, be inherited for a second life, provided that the heir discharged, or paid somebody else to discharge, the obligations of military service. Mendoza himself was expressly empowered to commend Indians. This change of policy significantly coincided with the foundation of Lima and the opening of another rich and populous continental area to Spanish exploitation. The concessions, presumably, were made in order to attract more settlers to the Indies. *Encomiendas* spread through the populous areas of Peru as quickly as they had done in New Spain, and the institution seemed to its beneficiaries to be accepted at last as a permanent feature of their society.

That the Emperor would see matters in this light was in the highest degree unlikely. Hapsburg persistence, Hapsburg tenacity of prerogative and principle, was certain in time to revert to standard traditional policy. The events of the early 1540's showed how far creole society had already diverged from the society of metropolitan Spain. The leading colonists were as blind to the motive forces of Spanish politics as Spanish statesmen were to the realities of colonial life. The colonial code of 1542, known as the New Laws of the Indies, with its drastic curtailment of settlers' privileges, both appalled and astonished those against whom it was directed, for there had been, in the Indies, no warning of a change of policy. In Spain, however, the indications of change had been accumulating for at least five years. Vitoria,[3] lecturing at Salamanca, had been subjecting the Spanish title to the Indies to destructive analysis. The Pope, Paul III, was persuaded by Spanish Dominican missionaries in 1537 to issue a series of bulls concerning the Indies. Of these, *Veritas ipsa* was a severe condemnation of Indian slavery; *Sublimis deus* condemned as heretical the opinion that the Indians were irrational and incapable of receiving the Faith. The Emperor, it is true, took exception on grounds of *Patronato* to the promulgation of these bulls in the Indies, but he did not disavow the principles which they proclaimed, and Las Casas and his friends distributed hundreds of copies before the royal prohibition could take effect. Las Casas himself—always at the centre of controversy, and with a reputation enormously enhanced by a successful

[3] ED. NOTE: Francisco de Vitoria, a sixteenth-century Dominican friar, renowned as a theologian and political theorist. He is now considered Spain's greatest contributor to international law.

mission in highland Guatemala—returned to Spain in 1539, and was one of the expert witnesses regularly consulted during the next three years by the Council which sat at Valladolid to draft the new code. Finally, and perhaps most important, reports of the violence and anarchy which followed the conquest of Peru were received by the Emperor with profound disquiet, and convinced him of the need for comprehensive legislation and drastic action to enforce royal authority.

The New Laws formed a comprehensive code—the first complete and adequate code—for the governance of all the provinces of the Indies. They were not, in general, revolutionary; they represented the traditional policy of the Crown. Most of their provisions duly came into force and were eventually included in the *Recopilación de Leyes*. Of the fifty-four articles of the code, twenty-three concerned native policy, and of these only four were seriously contentious: the four which dealt with *encomiendas* and slavery. After many years of shifts and equivocations the battle between Crown and settlers on these crucial issues was now to be fought in earnest. Articles 31 and 35 in effect abolished the *encomienda*. Some grants were to be terminated immediately, in particular those held by officials, those held by corporate bodies, such as town councils or monasteries, and those of individuals who had taken part in the recent disturbances in Peru. This last clause, if strictly interpreted, would have deprived almost every *encomendero* in Peru. All other *encomiendas* were to run to the death of their holders, and then to escheat to the Crown. Similarly, Indian slavery was to disappear within a generation. Indian women and children held as slaves were to be liberated at once. Male slaves whose slave status arose from lawful cause (such as capture in rebellion) were to remain in slavery, but all others were to be released, and the burden of proof was to rest on the owner. No Indians were to be enslaved for any reason in future.

The time was singularly inopportune for the promulgation of such a code. In New Spain the *encomienda* system had recently been put to a severe test as an organisation for defence. The Mixton rebellion of 1540-1, which originated among the half-subdued tribes of New Galicia, had spread to New Spain and seriously threatened the Spanish government there. The *encomenderos* of both kingdoms had been called out with their men, under the personal command of the viceroy. The rebellion had been put down by difficult mountain campaigns, in which a number of Spaniards, including the famous Alvarado, had been killed. The *encomenderos* of New Spain were in no mood to be deprived of the rewards of courage and loyalty. In Peru the distribution of *encomiendas* among the conquerors was barely completed. The *encomenderos* had lately been more concerned with cutting one another's throats than in fighting the Indians, but Manco Inca was still at large. Fresh fighting, whether between Spanish factions or against Indian risings, might break out at any time. Men slept with their weapons within reach, and might use them against a government which sought to take away their livelihood.

The Council of the Indies knew from experience that colonial officials, when ordered to enforce unpopular enactments, tended to temporise, to find excuses for evasion. To ensure enforcement on this critical occasion, they sent out, in 1544, special commissioners to each of the major centres of colonial government, with full powers to remove recalcitrant or venal officials. In New Spain the *visitador,* Tello de Sandoval, had the good sense to consult Mendoza, and was quickly convinced of the dangers of the situation. He agreed to postpone enforcement pending investigation, and the answers to his inquiries, from all classes of Spaniards, including the missionary clergy, showed a remarkable unanimity. The submission of the Dominicans, in particular, gives a vivid impression of the fears of the Spanish community, numbering only a few thousand, hemmed in by Indians who had largely lost their fear of European weapons, who were crowding into the Spanish settlements, and who effectively controlled the greater part of the colony's food supply. All the petitioners agreed that without *encomiendas* the settlers would desert or starve. In Peru events pursued a very different course. No settled royal administration existed there. The first viceroy was appointed, and the *audiencia* of Lima created at this time, with express orders to enforce the New Laws. Blasco Núñez' blind adherence to his instructions, as we have seen, provoked the armed insurrection of Gonzalo Pizarro, in which the viceroy himself was killed. This was the first major overt rebellion among New World Spaniards; it could be met in only one way: ruthless suppression, and the execution of the leaders. The skill of Pedro de la Gasca and the fears and factions of the rebels made this possible in 1548. Meanwhile, the existence of rebellion had stiffened the determination of the Crown to make its will effective. Instead of withdrawing its unpopular decrees in the face of resistance, as it had done on former occasions, the Council of the Indies looked for the minimum concessions which would make the New Laws enforceable without sacrificing any major principle. The results were embodied in a series of decrees between 1545 and 1549. The laws on Indian slavery were to stand, and were, within the next few years, substantially enforced, at least in New Spain and Guatemala. *Encomiendas,* on the other hand, were authorised once more, but with a vital difference: *encomenderos* were to be entitled only to the tributes of their Indians, tributes which at that time usually took the form of traditionally fixed amounts of maize, poultry, cotton cloth or *cacao.* They were forbidden to demand any form of labour or to claim any jurisdiction. In this way the central principles of the personal liberty of the Indians, and the direct control of the Crown over them, were preserved, while at the same time the 'old conquerors' and their descendants were assured of an income in consideration of their past exertions and their present liability to military service. This arrangement, with minor modifications, survived for many years. Perpetual inheritance, though often asked, was steadily refused. Only in rare and special instances were exceptions made. Two of Montezuma's daughters received Indian towns in perpetual *encomienda;* but the Cortés *marquesado* was the only perpetual hereditary *encomienda* ever granted to a Spaniard in the Indies.

Concessions were made: in New Spain a third 'life' was authorised in 1555, and a fourth in 1607. In Peru two lives remained the rule until 1629, when inheritance for a third was permitted in return for a money payment. *Encomiendas* were sometimes reassigned, especially in Peru, but more commonly they escheated, to be administered by *corregidores* on behalf of the Crown. In the 1550's and 1560's, the viceregal governments made determined efforts, through detailed *visitas* conducted by *audiencia* judges, to assess the tributes payable by all Indian towns, whether held by the Crown or by *encomenderos.* Miscellaneous and variable contributions in kind were commuted into fixed annual amounts of maize or money, known to the Indians. *Encomenderos* thus became a class of pensioners receiving, in theory, a fixed income. In fact, as a result of inflation and the decline of Indian numbers, their incomes steadily dwindled. From Philip IV's time, moreover, they became liable to a heavy, though intermittent, tax, the *media anata.* By the end of the sixteenth century the *encomienda* had ceased to be a major factor in the economy of the Indies. By the end of the seventeenth it had almost disappeared.

In its insistence on the personal liberty of the Indians the Crown had won a notable victory. As we have seen, however, liberty did not mean freedom to be idle. Colonies could not survive without labour, and the problem remained of inducing Indians to work for wages. During the dispute over the New Laws two events occurred which made this problem more acute than ever: the discovery of the silver veins of Potosí and Zacatecas greatly increased the demand for labour, and the disastrous epidemic of 1545 (in New Spain especially) greatly reduced the supply. One by one the Crown had prohibited the familiar methods of private compulsion in securing labour; it could not now avoid the use of public compulsion. A decree of 1549 required all unemployed Indians, whether tributary to the Crown or to *encomenderos,* to offer themselves for hire in the public places of their districts, 'without molestation or pressure except such as should be necessary to make them work.' They were to work for such employers as they chose, for a length of time agreed upon by free contract, and were to be paid wages according to a scale fixed by the viceroy or local governor. As might be expected, this naïve decree had little immediate effect, and certainly did not attract labour to the mines. A more specific form of compulsory recruitment was needed; and one was found in the system known in Peru (where it was inherited from the Incas) as *mita,* in New Spain as *repartimiento.* This was in essence a public *corvée.* It was not new; it had long been used in a casual and *ad hoc* fashion to recruit labour from the Crown *pueblos* for public works; but in the later sixteenth century it was made permanent, regular and general. Every settled Indian town or village, through its headmen, was required to send a fixed proportion of its male population out to work, for a fixed number of weeks, in rotation throughout the year. The labourers so recruited were allocated, by a local magistrate known as the *juez repartidor,* to works for which *repartimiento* labour had been authorised. Public works—roads, bridges, public buildings—together with churches, convents and hospitals, usually had first claim; but silver-mining counted as a public purpose for *repartimiento* labour, at the discretion of the colonial authorities, and *repartimientos* might also be authorised for large-scale manufactures, such as cloth and sugar, for estate labour and for porterage. Wages were payable, at rates fixed by the colonial authorities; as might be expected, the rates were low. Employers in favoured industries thus gained a cheap and regular but constantly changing labour force; Indians were compelled, for a part of every year, to do uncongenial work in strange surroundings, often far from home; and the villages lost a proportion of the men available for communal farming, so that those left at home had to work harder in order to live and to meet the continuing, inexorable demand for tribute.

The use of *repartimiento* labour was a privilege for which an express administrative order was in theory required in each instance. Such orders could be granted by viceroys, governing *audiencias,* or in New Spain by the *Juzgado general de Indios,* a special court of summary jurisdiction set up, after the second great epidemic of 1576, to deal with Indian affairs. The liability of villages to provide labour was assessed by the same authorities. The assessments, infrequently revised, tended to grow into bodies of local custom as complex as those which in former times had governed labour dues in the villages of Europe. In 1609, however, the Council of the Indies made a determined attempt to codify the rules, and the legislation of that year, with minor modifications, remained in force for some 200 years. The quota of men required from each village at any one time was limited to one-seventh of the male population; or for work in the mines, 4 per cent. Casual gang labour was unsuitable for the skilled and semi-skilled work of mining, and mine-owners were prepared to pay relatively high wages to skilled Indian employees. For pick-and-shovel work they preferred to employ Negro slaves, when they could get them. The Crown encouraged this, partly to lighten the burden of forced labour on the Indians, and partly to increase the revenue from the import duty on slaves. *Repartimiento* gangs were certainly used in mining—the Potosí mines had a particularly evil reputation as devourers of *mitayos*—but only for lack of slaves or free wage-earners. *Repartimiento* labour was prohibited, by the 1609 code, in certain arduous or unhealthy occupations: in sugar-mills, in textile workshops, in pearl-fishing and in the operation of hand pumps for draining mine shafts. These, presumably, were jobs for slaves or convicts; though in the seventeenth century the hand pump for draining mines was often replaced by the animal-powered whim or *malacate*. The employment of Indians as porters, save in certain special circumstances, was also forbidden. By this time, mules were plentiful enough to make such a rule reasonable, though not necessarily enforceable; in practice porters continued to carry burdens; in some places they still do. Spanish traders often complained that their Indian competitors, unfettered by sentimental prejudice, continued to employ porters and gained an unfair advantage by so doing, but official opinion remained adamant, using free men as beasts of burden. Agriculture and cattle-herding, on the other hand, were considered highly suitable occupations for Indians. Spanish-owned estates in the later sixteenth century relied heavily on *repartimiento* labour. Viceroys were given a wide discretion to vary the legal quotas, and naturally the heaviest demands came at the periods of the farming year when labour was most needed on the Indians' own land.

The obligation to provide labour rested not on the individual Indian but on the *pueblo,* the town or village to which he belonged. It must be remembered that forced labour was not only an economic convenience for the Spanish settlers; it was regarded also as part of a civilising, Hispanicising process. For Spaniards, civilised life meant urban life; and so the inculcation of regular habits of work was associated in the official mind with the creation of a properly organised urban polity for the Indians. Many Indians, of course, already lived in concentrated settlements before the conquest. In these settlements the object of colonial policy was to make urban government conform as closely as possible to the pattern familiar in Spanish towns; to replace the traditional authority of headmen or *caciques*—who were often custodians of sacred ritual rather than political leaders—by town councils of Spanish type; to induce the councils to elect magistrates and constables, who should be responsible to the local Spanish governors for the collection of the tribute, the organisation of labour and the maintenance of the peace. For those Indians—in some areas the great majority—who lived scattered among their fields, a more radical policy was devised for 'congregating' them in towns or villages planned on Spanish lines from the beginning. The Mendicant friars, as we have seen, early adopted this policy in order to facilitate their missionary work. In the second half of the sixteenth century as Mendicant influence in the settled areas declined, the task of congregating the Indians was taken over by the civil authorities; though, of course, the building of a church and the provision of a priest were essential features of any new settlement. In Peru an extensive resettlement of scattered Indians was carried out by the viceroy Francisco de Toledo in the 1570's. The most ambitious 'congregation' was that undertaken in New Spain, after repeated prodding from Madrid, by Luis de Velasco II and the Conde de Monterey at the end of the sixteenth century and the beginning of the seventeenth. This operation covered the whole of settled New Spain and New Galicia. Apart from considerations of general policy, the depopulation of the viceroyalty by successive epidemics had made a concentration of the surviving population urgently necessary. Usually existing townships formed the nuclei of congregations, and received the people displaced from nearby hamlets; but some entirely new villages took root and are thriving communities today—evidence of the care with which their sites were selected. Some were deliberately planted—for obvious reasons—in the neighbourhood of mining settlements. The resettlement undoubtedly involved an immense upheaval in the life of the Indians concerned. The commissioners' instructions forbade them to use force in moving people into the new settlement; but most Indians, imbued with conservative traditions and an instinctive love of the soil, would not have moved willingly. The only contemporary general account of the proceedings is that contained in Torquemada's *Monarquía Indiana*. Torquemada was a friar, and a hostile witness. His evidence, like that of Las Casas in an earlier generation, must be treated with caution; but he was probably not far from the truth when he asserted that Indians were compelled to move to new homes chiefly by the deliberate destruction of their old ones.

The supervision of Indian communities, old and new, with the task of encouraging their members to adopt Spanish habits, techniques and forms of government, was entrusted to a staff of district officers known as *corregidores*. In the second half of the sixteenth century these officials took over the social responsibilities—not, of course, the military responsibilities—which in earlier years had been left to *encomenderos*. Spanish legislation tended to assume, somewhat uncritically, that paid officials would always be more conscientious and more effective agents of the royal will than private feudatories. In the local government of the Indies this assumption was not always valid. There were two quite distant kinds of *corregidor*. The *corregidor* of a Spanish town—in Spain or in the Indies—was the representative there of royal authority, a magistrate and a professional administrator of considerable dignity and power. Usually he was a trained lawyer. *Corregidores de Indios,* on the other hand, were amateurs selected usually from among settlers who had no *encomienda* or landed estates, and therefore no ready source of income. They had no particular training for their duties. They were appointed for short periods, usually two or three years, and were paid a small salary charged upon the local tributes. Inevitably they tended to regard their office as a personal perquisite, and to make the most of it while it lasted. The *corregimiento* was one of the least efficient and least reliable institutions of colonial government. Never adequately supervised, it could be made the excuse for a petty local tyranny more burdensome than the *encomienda* had ever been. As Torquemada sourly explained, the *corregidor* robbed in order to return rich to Spain; the *cacique* robbed to keep the *corregidor* quiet.

The whole system of native administration invited abuse. Our knowledge of its operation in New Spain comes mainly from the records of the *Juzgado general de Indios,* the vigorous summary court before which most of the disputes which arose were heard. The commonest complaints were of labour demands in excess of those permitted by law; of *corregidores* who extorted labour and tribute for their own private use; of headmen who used their powers of coercion to extort bribes or pay off grudges; of employers who withheld wages, seized the possession of the Indians to prevent them from running away, or kept them beyond the authorised time; of trespass by Spanish flocks and herds on Indian fields; of occasional physical ill-treatment. The *Juzgado* was remarkable, by seventeenth-century standards, for its accessibility to Indian petitioners and for the despatch with which it handled their complaints; but thousands of complaints never reached it. In Peru there was no *Juzgado,* and petitions had to go through the complicated and dilatory procedure of the *audiencias.* Throughout the Indies, legislation intended to soften the impact of forced labour and to protect recognised Indian interest lost effectiveness and force through lack of adequate local supervision.

The social abuses and the economic wastefulness of the forced labour system were well known to responsible officials and to the Council of the Indies. They were tolerated partly because there was no obvious alternative, partly because the *repartimiento* was regarded, as the old *encomi-*

enda had been, as a temporary makeshift, until Indian society could be reshaped in a European mould. For the individual Indian the only way of escape from the alternating compulsions of *repartimiento* and village community was to accept the implications of a money economy, move to a Spanish settlement, put on European clothes and become a wage-earner, or, if his resources and skill allowed, a craftsman or small capitalist. This, of course, was what Spanish legislators considered to be the ultimate and sensible outcome.

The French, the English, and the Indians

FRANCIS PARKMAN

In this essay, Francis Parkman, a brilliant nineteenth-century historian and prolific interpreter of French America, compares French and British Indian policy. Initially he uses his considerable descriptive talents to narrate the vicissitudes of New France in the Iroquois War, but he then goes on to discuss reasons why the Canadians achieved so much success among the Indians. Parkman argues that good relations were essential for a profitable fur trade, that the "pliant and plastic temper" of the French was particularly suited to friendly intercourse with the indigenes, and that Canada's geographical position made it easy for the *coureurs de bois* to penetrate the interior. Implicit is an emphasis, lacking in the selections by McRae and Diamond, upon the importance of the fur trade to Canada's economic health. Implicit, too, but starkly evident after reading Parry's description of Spanish policy, is the immense contrast between the Indian problems faced by governors of Spanish America and by those of English and French America.

With a pro-French bias, Parkman disparages English Indian policy. Looking behind his criticisms, however, one may suggest that the uncoordinated—and

From Francis Parkman, *History of the Conspiracy of Pontiac, and the War of the North American Tribes Against the English Colonies after the Conquest of Canada,* Boston: Little, Brown and Company, 1855, pp. 59-71.

for Parkman—unsuccessful English Indian program was an inevitable con-
comitant of the whole permissive scheme of English colonization. Whether
this policy would have remained so uncoordinated had the fur trade become
as important to the English colonies as to New France is, of course, a crucial
question. In New York and the extreme southern colonies, where the British
were most successful among the natives, settlers participated enthusiastically
in the fur trade and profited from it. But over-all the Indian problem was less
important for British colonists than for those of New France, and much less
so than for Spanish America.

THE FRENCH COLONISTS OF CANADA HELD, FROM THE BEGINNING, A
peculiar intimacy of relation with the Indian tribes. With the English colonists it was far otherwise; and the difference sprang from
several causes. The fur-trade was the life of Canada; agriculture and commerce were the chief fountains of wealth to the British provinces. The
Romanish zealots of Canada burned for the conversion of the heathen;
their heretic rivals were fired with no such ardor. And finally, while the
ambition of France grasped at empire over the farthest deserts of the west,
the steady industry of the English colonist was contented to cultivate and
improve a narrow strip of seaboard. Thus it happened that the farmer of
Massachusetts and the Virginian planter were conversant with only a few
bordering tribes, while the priests and emissaries of France were roaming
the prairies with the buffalo-hunting Pawnees, or lodging in the winter
cabins of the Dahcotah; and swarms of savages, whose uncouth names
were strange to English ears, descended yearly from the north, to bring
their beaver and otter skins to the market of Montreal.

The position of Canada invited intercourse with the interior, and
eminently favored her schemes of commerce and policy. The River St.
Lawrence, and the chain of the great lakes, opened a vast extent of
inland navigation; while their tributary streams, interlocking with the
branches of the Mississippi, afforded ready access to that mighty river,
and gave the restless voyager free range over half the continent. But
these advantages were well nigh neutralized. Nature opened the way, but
a watchful and terrible enemy guarded the portal. The forests south of
Lake Ontario gave harborage to the five tribes of the Iroquois, implaca-
ble foes of Canada. They waylaid her trading parties, routed her soldiers,
murdered her missionaries, and spread havoc and woe through all her
settlements.

It was an evil hour for Canada, when, on the twenty-eighth of May,
1609, Samuel de Champlain, impelled by his own adventurous spirit,
departed from the hamlet of Quebec to follow a war-party of Algonquins

against their hated enemy, the Iroquois. Ascending the Sorel, and passing the rapids at Chambly, he embarked on the lake which bears his name, and with two French attendants, steered southward, with his savage associates, toward the rocky promontory of Ticonderoga. They moved with all the precaution of Indian warfare; when, at length as night was closing in, they descried a band of the Iroquois in their large canoes of elm bark approaching through the gloom. Wild yells from either side announced the mutual discovery. Both parties hastened to the shore, and all night long the forest resounded with their discordant war-songs and fierce whoops of defiance. Day dawned, and the fight began. Bounding from tree to tree, the Iroquois pressed forward to the attack; but when Champlain advanced from among the Algonquins, and stood full in sight before them, with his strange attire, his shining breastplate, and features unlike their own; when they saw the flash of his arquebuse, and beheld two of their chiefs fall dead, they could not contain their terror, but fled for shelter into the depths of the wood. The Algonquins pursued, slaying many in the fight, and the victory was complete.

Such was the first collision between the white men and the Iroquois; and Champlain flattered himself that the latter had learned for the future to respect the arms of France. He was fatally deceived. The Iroquois recovered from their terrors, but they never forgave the injury; and yet it would be unjust to charge upon Champlain the origin of the desolating wars which were soon to scourge the colony. The Indians of Canada, friends and neighbors of the French, had long been harassed by inroads of the fierce confederates, and under any circumstances the French must soon have become parties to the quarrel.

Whatever may have been its origin, the war was fruitful of misery to the youthful colony. The passes were beset by ambushed war-parties. The routes between Quebec and Montreal were watched with tigerlike vigilance. Bloodthirsty warriors prowled about the outskirts of the settlements. Again and again the miserable people, driven within the palisades of their forts, looked forth upon wasted harvests and blazing roofs. The Island of Montreal was swept with fire and steel. The fur-trade was interrupted, since for months together all communication was cut off with the friendly tribes of the west. Agriculture was checked; the fields lay fallow, and frequent famine was the necessary result. The name of the Iroquois became a by-word of horror through the colony, and to the suffering Canadians they seemed no better than troops of incarnate fiends. Revolting rites and monstrous superstitions were imputed to them; and, among the rest, it was currently believed that they cherished the custom of immolating young children, burning them with fire, and drinking the ashes mixed with water to increase their bravery. Yet the wildest imaginations could scarcely exceed the truth. At the attack of Montreal, they placed infants over the embers, and forced the wretched mothers to turn the spit; and those who fell within their clutches endured torments too hideous for description. Their ferocity was equalled only by their courage and address.

At intervals, the afflicted colony found respite from its suffering; and through the efforts of the Jesuits, fair hopes began to rise of propitiating the terrible foe. At one time, the influence of the priests availed so far, that under their auspices a French colony was formed in the very heart of the Iroquois country; but the settlers were soon forced to a precipitate flight, and the war broke out afresh. The French, on their part, were not idle; they faced their assailants with characteristic gallantry. Courcelles, Tracy, De la Barre, and De Nonville invaded by turns, with various success, the forest haunts of the confederates; and at length, in the year 1696, the veteran Count Frontenac marched upon their cantons with all the force of Canada. Stemming the surges of La Chine, sweeping through the romantic channels of the Thousand Islands, and over the glimmering surface of Lake Ontario, and, trailing in long array up the current of the Oswego, they disembarked on the margin of the Lake of Onondaga, and, startling the woodland echoes with the unwonted clangor of their trumpets, urged their perilous march through the mazes of the forest. Never had those solitudes beheld so strange a pageantry. The Indian allies, naked to the waist and horribly painted, adorned with streaming scalp-locks and fluttering plumes, stole crouching among the thickets, or peered with lynx-eyed vision through the labyrinths of foliage. Scouts and forest-rangers scoured the woods in front and flank of the marching columns—men trained among the hardships of the fur-trade, thin, sinewy, and strong arrayed in wild costume of beaded moc-cason, scarlet leggin, and frock of buckskin, fantastically garnished with many-colored embroidery of porcupine. Then came the levies of the colony, in gray capotes and gaudy sashes, and the trained battalions from old France in burnished cuirass and head-piece, veterans of European wars. Plumed cavaliers were there, who had followed the standards of Condé or Turenne, and who, even in the depths of wilderness, scorned to lay aside the martial foppery which bedecked the camp and court of Louis the Magnificent. The stern commander was borne along upon a litter in the midst, his locks bleached with years, but his eyes kindling with the quenchless fire which, like a furnace burned hottest when its fuel was almost spent. Thus, beneath the sepulchral arches of the forest, through tangled thickets, and over prostrate trunks, the aged nobleman advanced to wreak his vengeance upon empty wigwams and deserted maize-fields.

Even the fierce courage of the Iroquois began to quail before these repeated attacks, while the gradual growth of the colony, and the arrival of troops from France, at length convinced them that they could not destroy Canada. With the opening of the eighteenth century, their rancor showed signs of abating: and in the year 1726, by dint of skilful intrigue, the French succeeded in erecting a permanent military post at the important pass of Niagara, within the limits of the confederacy. Meanwhile, in spite of every obstacle, the power of France had rapidly extended its boundaries in the west. French influence diffused itself through a thousand channels, among distant tribes, hostile, for the most part, to the domineering Iroquois. Forts, mission-houses, and armed trading stations secured the principal passes. Traders, and *coureurs des bois* pushed their adventurous traffic into the wildest deserts; and French guns and hatchets, French beads and cloth, French tobacco and brandy, were known from where the stunted Esquimaux burrowed in their snow caves, to where the Camanches scoured the plains of the south with their banditti cavalry. Still this far-extended commerce continued to advance westward. In 1738, La Verandrye essayed to reach those mysterious mountains which, as the Indians alleged, lay beyond the arid deserts of the Missouri and the Saskatchawan. Indian hostility defeated his enterprise, but not before he had struck far out into these unknown wilds, and formed a line of trading posts, one of which, Fort de la Reine, was planted on the Assinniboin, a hundred leagues beyond Lake Winnipeg. At that early period, France left her footsteps upon the dreary wastes which even now have no other tenants than the Indian buffalo-hunter or the roving trapper.

The fur-trade of the English colonist opposed but feeble rivalry to that of their hereditary foes. At an early period, favored by the friendship of the Iroquois, they attempted to open a traffic with the Algonquin tribes of the great lakes; and in the year 1687, Major McGregory ascended with a boat-load of goods to Lake Huron, where his appearance excited great commotion and where he was promptly seized and imprisoned by a party of the French. From this time forward, the English fur-trade languished, until the year 1725, when Governor Burnet, of New York, established a post on Lake Ontario, at the mouth of the River Oswego, whither, lured by the cheapness and excellence of the English goods, crowds of savages soon congregated from every side, to the unspeakable annoyance of the French. Meanwhile, a considerable commerce was springing up with the Cherokees and other tribes of the south; and during the first half of the century, the people of Pennsylvania began to cross the Alleghanies, and carry on a lucrative traffic with the tribes of the Ohio. In 1749, La Jonquiere, the governor of Canada, learned, to his great indignation, that several English traders had reached Sandusky, and were exerting a bad influence upon the Indians of that quarter; and two years later, he caused four of the intruders to be seized near the Ohio, and sent prisoners to Canada.

These early efforts of the English, considerable as they were, can ill bear comparison with the vast extent of the French interior commerce. In respect also to missionary enterprise, and the political influence resulting from it, the French had every advantage over rivals whose zeal for conversion was neither kindled by fanaticism nor fostered by an ambitious government. Eliot labored within call of Boston, while the heroic Brebeuf faced the ghastly perils of the western wilderness; and the wanderings of Brainerd sink into insignificance compared with those of the devoted Rasles. Yet, in judging the relative merits of the Romish and Protestant missionaries, it must not be forgotten that while the former contented themselves with sprinkling a few drops of water on the forehead of the warlike proselyte, the latter sought to wean him from his barbarism, and penetrate his savage heart with the truths of Christianity.

In respect, also, to direct political influence, the advantage was wholly on the side of France. The English colonies, broken into separate governments, were incapable of exercising a vigorous and consistent Indian policy; and the measures of one government often clashed with those of another. Even in the separate provinces, the popular nature of the constitution and the quarrels of governors and assemblies were unfavorable to efficient action; and this was more especially the case in the province of New York, where the vicinity of the Iroquois rendered strenuous yet prudent measures of the utmost importance. The powerful confederates, hating the French with bitter enmity, naturally inclined to the English alliance; and a proper treatment would have secured their firm and lasting friendship. But, at the early periods of her history, the assembly of New York was made up in great measure of narrow-minded men, more eager to consult their own petty immediate interests than to pursue any farsighted scheme of public welfare. Other causes conspired to injure the British interest in this quarter. The annual present sent from England to the Iroquois was often embezzled by corrupt governors or their favorites. The proud chiefs were disgusted by the cold and haughty bearing of the English officials, and a pernicious custom prevailed of conducting Indian negotiations through the medium of the fur-traders, a class of men held in contempt by the Iroquois, and known among them by the significant title of "rum-carriers." In short, through all the counsels of the province, Indian affairs were grossly and madly neglected.

With more or less emphasis, the same remark holds true of all the other English colonies. With those of France, it was far otherwise; and this difference between the rival powers was naturally incident to their different forms of government, and different conditions of development. France labored with eager diligence to conciliate the Indians, and win them to espouse her cause. Her agents were busy in every village, studying the language of the inmates, complying with their usages, flattering their prejudices, caressing them, cajoling them, and whispering friendly warnings in their ears against the wicked designs of the English. When a party of Indian chiefs visited a French fort, they were greeted with the firing of cannon and rolling of drums; they were regaled at the tables of the officers, and bribed with medals and decorations, scarlet uniforms and French flags. Far wiser than their rivals, the French never ruffled the self-complacent dignity of their guests, never insulted their religious notions, nor ridiculed their ancient customs. They met the savage halfway, and showed an abundant readiness to mould their own features after his likeness. Count Frontenac himself, plumed and painted like an Indian chief, danced the war-dance and yelled the war-song at the campfires of his delighted allies. It would have been well had the French been less exact in their imitations, for at times they copied their model with infamous fidelity, and fell into excesses scarcely credible but for the concurrent testimony of their own writers. Frontenac caused an Iroquois prisoner to be burnt alive to strike terror into his countrymen; and Louvigny, French commandant at Michillimackinac, in 1695, tortured an Iroquois ambassador to death, that he might break off a negotiation between that people and the Wyandots. Nor are these the only well attested instances of each execrable inhumanity. But if the French were guilty of these cruelties against their Indian enemies, they were no less guilty of unworthy compliance with the demands of their Indian friends, in cases where Christianity and civilization would have dictated a prompt refusal. Even the brave Montcalm stained his bright name by abandoning the hapless defenders of Oswego and William Henry to the tender mercies of an Indian mob.

In general, however, the Indian policy of the French cannot be charged with obsequiousness. Complaisance was tempered with dignity. At an early period, they discerned the peculiarities of the native character, and clearly saw that, while, on the one hand, it was necessary to avoid giving offence, it was not less necessary, on the other, to assume a bold demeanor and a show of power; to caress with one hand, and grasp a drawn sword with the other. Every crime against a Frenchman was promptly chastised by the sharp agency of military law; while among the English, the offender could only be reached through the medium of the civil courts, whose delays, uncertainties, and evasions excited the wonder and provoked the contempt of the Indians.

It was by observance of the course indicated above—a course highly judicious in a political point of view, whatever it may have been to the eye of the moralist—that the French were enabled to maintain themselves in small detached posts, far aloof from the parent colony and environed by barbarous tribes, where an English garrison would have been cut off in a twelvemonth. They professed to hold these posts, not in their own right, but purely through the grace and condescension of the surrounding savages; and by this conciliating assurance they sought to make good their position, until, with their growing strength, conciliation should no more be needed.

In its efforts to win the friendship and alliance of the Indian tribes, the French government found every advantage in the peculiar character of its subjects—that pliant and plastic temper which forms so marked a contrast to the stubborn spirit of the Englishman. From the beginning, the French showed a tendency to amalgamate with the forest tribes. "The manners of the savages," writes the Baron La Hontan, "are perfectly agreeable to my palate," and many a restless adventurer, of high or low degree, might have echoed the words of the erratic soldier. At first, great hopes were entertained that, by the mingling of French and Indians, the latter would be won over to civilization and the church; but the effect was precisely the reverse; for, as Charlevoix observes, the savages did not become French, but the French became savages. Hundreds betook themselves to the forest, never more to return. These outflowings of French civilization were merged in the waste of barbarism, as a river is lost in the sands of the desert. The wandering Frenchman chose a wife or a concubine among his Indian friends; and, in a few generations, scarcely a tribe of the west was free from an infusion of Celtic blood. The French empire in America could exhibit among its subjects every shade of color from white to red, every gradation of culture from the highest civilization of Paris to the rudest barbarism of the wigwam.

The fur-trade engendered a peculiar class of men known by the appropriate name of bush-rangers, or *coureurs des bois,* half-civilized vagrants, whose chief vocation was conducting the canoes of the traders along the lakes and rivers of the interior: many of them, however, shaking loose every tie of blood and kindred, identified themselves with the Indians, and sank into utter barbarism. In many a squalid camp among the plains and forests of the west, the traveller would have encountered men owning the blood and speaking the language of France, yet, in their wild and swarthy visages and barbarous costume, seeming more akin to those with whom they had cast their lot. The renegade of civilization caught the habits and imbibed the prejudices of his chosen associates. He loved to decorate his long hair with eagle feathers, to make his face hideous with vermilion, ochre, and soot, and to adorn his greasy hunting frock with horsehair fringes. His dwelling, if he had one, was a wigwam. He lounged on a bear-skin while his squaw boiled his venison and lighted his pipe. In hunting, in dancing, in singing, in taking a scalp, he rivalled the genuine Indian. His mind was tinctured with the superstitions of the forest. He had faith in the magic drum of the conjurer; he was not sure that a thunder cloud could not be frightened away by whistling at it through the wing bone of an eagle; he carried the tail of a rattlesnake in his bullet pouch by way of amulet; and he placed implicit trust in the prophetic truth of his dreams. This class of men is not yet extinct In the cheerless wilds beyond the northern lakes, or among the mountain solitudes of the distant west, they may still be found, unchanged in life and character since the day when Louis the Great claimed sovereignty over this desert empire.

The borders of the English colonies displayed no such phenomena of mingling races; for here a thorny and impracticable barrier divided the white man from the red. The English fur-traders, and the rude men in their employ, showed, it is true, an ample alacrity to fling off the restraints of civilization; but though they became barbarians, they did not become Indians; and scorn on the one side, and hatred on the other, still marked the intercourse of the hostile races. With the settlers of the frontier it was much the same. Rude, fierce, and contemptuous, they daily encroached upon the hunting-grounds of the Indians, and then paid them for the injury with abuse and insult, curses and threats. Thus the native population shrank back from before the English, as from before an advancing pestilence; while, on the other hand, in the very heart of Canada, Indian communities sprang up, cherished by the government, and favored by the easy-tempered people. At Lorette, at Caughnawaga, at St. Francis, and elsewhere within the province, large bands were gathered together, consisting in part of fugitives from the borders of the hated English, and aiding, in time of war, to swell the forces of the French in repeated forays against the settlements of New York and New England.

COLONIAL CULTURE AND LEARNING: SPANISH AND ENGLISH AMERICA IN THE EIGHTEENTH CENTURY

Spanish American Culture: The University of San Carlos de Guatemala in the Eighteenth Century

JOHN TATE LANNING

The societies of the Spanish and British empires, in so many ways at opposite poles, had in common a vigorous, scientific elite. For some with a strong Anglo-Saxon bias, writes Professor John Tate Lanning, James B. Duke Professor of History at Duke University and author of this selection, the strength of the Enlightenment in the Spanish colonies may come as a surprise; but the evidence is imposing and his discussion convincing. For good reason he has based his study on the University of San Carlos de Guatemala; it is the only major university of colonial Spanish America for which there is sufficient documentary evidence for close analysis.

The enthusiastic reception given the Scientific Revolution and the intellectual vigor of the professors at San Carlos is not all that emerges from Professor Lanning's account. He shows also—again, surprisingly, to some—that neither the heavy hand of the Inquisition nor the obscurantism of clerics or scholastic academics retarded the flowering of the new learning partly because, until the eve of the colonial revolt against Spain, imperial administrators saw the value of scientific inquiry.

Lanning's catalog of the accomplishments of the scholars at San Carlos may profitably be compared with the English experience described in the next selection. For the most part the same currents flowed through the cultural life of both areas, although Lanning's comments on the attitude of the professors toward the first signs of revolutionary discontent hint at the effect of social stratification described by Professor Leonard. Above all, Lanning's essay highlights the fact that Spanish American scholars, like those in the thirteen colonies, had awakened from the long "noonday nap" of the baroque epoch to break with Peripateticism and Scholasticism and opened the way for the ideas of the Scientific Revolution and the Enlightenment.

U NTIL THIS GENERATION, IF NOT UNTIL THIS MOMENT, TRADITION outside the Iberian Peninsula has had it that Spain's Empire lived in sleepy isolation and that her colonial policy was one of steadfast opposition to enlightenment. Edward Jenner,[1] who thought that the Spaniards would be the "last people" to take up smallpox vaccination "with any degree of ardor," joyfully admitted, though he could not conceal his astonishment, that they were "in reality among Europeans the first." In 1800 a Scotchman or a Frenchman could be found to testify that learning in the Spanish Empire was "three hundred years behind," but since the historians take the most damaging testimony against a people "out of their own mouths," they have Charles IV demanding to know what the Venezuelans want with universities when it is merely "the duty of vassals to obey and be silent." This remark is too glib, too well adapted to the unconscious depreciation of Spain running through modern history, to be plausible, even on the lips of an imbecile king tinkering with his

From John Tate Lanning, *The Eighteenth-Century Enlightenment in the University of San Carlos de Guatemala,* Ithaca: Cornell University Press, 1956, pp. 342-356. © 1956 by Cornell University. Used by permission of Cornell University Press.

[1] ED. NOTE: Edward Jenner, discoverer of smallpox vaccine.

clocks or pouting about the infidelities of the queen. It is easy, sometimes irresistibly easy, to sully the proud name of Conquistador with telling quotation and eyewitness authority, but nothing could be fairer to the critics than to let the historic bias of the Anglo-Saxon race dangle on a clause of Jenner's: "The Spaniards whom one would have thought would have been the last people."

ISOLATION

The case of Guatemala will show how false is the assumption that the Spanish Empire was intellectually isolated and deliberately kept in ignorance by Madrid. The new learning was enthusiastically received here at least two decades before the French Revolution began. When Goicoechea[2] gave up his chair in the Franciscan Convent to teach experimental, Newtonian physics in San Carlos after the expulsion of the Jesuits in 1767, he had 74 students in that one class—six more than the largest graduating class in the history of the University and four more than the total student body when the University was founded. The individual professor and the religious order, when called upon to testify about the University in 1782, offered this change as evidence that the institution was sound—sure proof that they had long known of the changes and approved of them in advance. They did not sound a single hostile note.

Theses covering the whole range of humanistic and scientific studies proclaim the decline and death of Peripateticism[3] not only in the academic vanguard but in the ranks. They show that the student studied every thinker of importance from Descartes to Kant and took over many of their doctrines. Though a good scholastic, we need to remind ourselves, always preferred "right reason" as the door to truth, weary commentators, lazy professors, and indifferent students were wont to raise up authority in its place. But, stimulated by the Enlightenment, professor and student began by disavowing authority, even that of the Holy Fathers, as alone adequate support for truth.

The denial of authority in philosophy had its counterpart in science. Students offered experiment in itself, not just lessons experimentally treated, as "a clearer method" of deciphering nature than logic-chopping.

---

[2] ED. NOTE: José Antonio Goicoechea, a learned and enlightened Franciscan, who introduced experimental physics into the University of San Carlos when he was asked to teach philosophy there after the expulsion of the Jesuits.

[3] ED. NOTE: The Aristotelian system of knowledge and teaching.

With the cleavage between the two approaches to knowledge of the physical world already reached in the University of San Carlos de Guatemala in 1770, students tried to get their new bearings and to clarify the problems of nature. Copernicus, when his name was first mentioned, was accepted so casually as to suggest that his system was nothing new. Newton, so coldly scientific and demonstrable as to escape the paganism of Aristotle and the infidelity of Locke,[4] was not so much quoted as chanted. An avid interest in earthquakes, tides, magnetic deflection, the aurora borealis, lightning and thunder, snow, and even animal freaks marked the "age of Philosophers." After Franklin sent his kite aloft, electricity became the physical phenomenon that provoked experiment and led at least one Guatemalan to seek out the great Galvani[5] himself. Heat and light underwent study that suggested and then proved the falsity of the ancient "elements." Newton refracted white light into its component colors, but University men wisely admitted that they did not know what light was nor how it traveled. In the days so soon after the student had been a mere scholastic and the professor, at best, a savant, openmindedness was especially wholesome.

The basic moves from Hippocratic to twentieth-century medicine, though naturally not all the important discoveries, were made by doctors from the University of San Carlos in the age of the Enlightenment.[6] Essential medical literature, without restriction, flowed in from Spain, England, Scotland, France, Holland, Germany, and Italy. In medicine there was, considering the scarcity of doctors in the kingdom, a surprising originality, flair for scholarship, and even inventiveness. Ávalos y Porras taught the circulation of the blood experimentally. Flores claimed as his creation the first wax anatomical figure in history that could be taken apart and reassembled. Linen and cotton loops, introduced into midwifery by the ancient Greeks, became wet, limp, and unmanageable in difficult deliveries, but Esparragosa overcame these defects by supplying a fabric personally woven of whale bristles for the "elastic" obstetrical forceps he perfected. He undertook delicate new operations on the eye in a scholarly rather than a commercial mood. It is doubtful if such large-scale and successful person-to-person smallpox inoculations took place anywhere in America as those performed by Flores more than twenty years before vaccination was possible. In the City, as soon as the

[4] ED. NOTE: John Locke (1632-1704), the English philosopher and political theorist, who is probably known best for his natural law theory to justify representative government and revolution.

[5] ED. NOTE: Luigi Galvani (1739-1798), Italian discoverer of dynamic electricity.

[6] ED. NOTE: The names mentioned in this paragraph were all professors of medicine in the University of San Carlos: Manuel Trinidad de Ávalos y Porras, José Felipe Flores, Narciso Esparragosa y Gallardo.

"inefable preservativo" arrived, Esparragosa vaccinated with a thoroughness to put to shame Boston, Philadelphia, or Charleston. The medical students were the first to abandon Latin as the language of their theses. After he had traveled in Europe, Flores thought that his "faculty" in Guatemala was not retarded and, with respect to method, could set the standard. At the end of colonial days, the dispute between the College of Surgery and the University of San Carlos showed that everybody involved knew that, aside from the amazing achievements of the overworked university elite, the kingdom at large was miserably served in medicine. The mumbo jumbo of oracular, bookish medicine was in disrepute and the country was mentally ready for everything the science of healing had to offer.

Thus, modernism was dominant in philosophy, science, and medicine. Those who had to hang their heads and speak, if they spoke at all, through the gawky scion of some rich family like the Ayzinenas were the two or three die-hards in the cloister. When the Dominican Luis de Escoto had his students go back to ante-Newtonian doctrines, he was as out of place in San Carlos as William Jennings Bryan in the role of director of the Museum of Natural History, Section Dinosauria. His colleagues bitterly opposed swearing him in as professor of philosophy—an indignity never suffered by any critic of "Aristotelian obscurantism." As a correspondent of the *Gazeta de Guatemala* tells a fellow pretending to be an old priest, and signing himself "Deceived," any man his age still not knowing about the progress in the arts and sciences, both in America and in Europe, deserved to be made a fool of.

In this transition from one set of ideas to another, the Guatemalan student was not so utterly taken in as were many in Europe and some in other Spanish colonies. It took the findings of a solemn report of the Louvre Society to the Medical Society of Paris to put at rest the fervent hope that smallpox vaccine would somehow overcome such troubles as menstruation and menopause. Flores in Guatemala contrived his paste of newts in the same spirit as Bartolache in Mexico concocted his martial pills—all, naturally, of unlimited curative powers. But this is the only project among the "Latin" physicians of the Kingdom of Guatemala not in the best clinical and research tradition.

Like any Spanish colonial, the Guatemalan was protected from these excesses by two things. The first of these, the self-assured European thesis that the mind had deteriorated in the New World, put well informed American students on their guard against the indiscriminate acceptance of ready-packed ideas. The second, the eclectic spirit that characterized the enlightened Spaniard everywhere, is best illustrated in the temperate reception of Descartes. Students accepted his "methodical doubt," but readily, even summarily, rejected his system as a whole. They never dreamed of taking his "vortexes" seriously, and while the problem of how the "soul" acted upon the body (the famous Cartesian dualism) still troubled them, they made short shrift of the pineal gland as the blending agent. In the same spirit they did not, as some did in Caracas and Lima, indulge in intemperate abuse of Aristotle because he symbolized the old system. Like the mosquito puncturing at random, they put in their sampling tubes and sucked up good wine where they found it regardless of vintage.[7]

The case of Guatemala also exposes the myth that any scientific or literary man, especially one capable of leading a revolution, had to go to Europe to get a university education, to sharpen his mind in the salons of the Enlightenment, or to gain inspiration from historic places. Miranda and Bolívar, wandering over the face of Europe, and San Martín, commanding a company in the Spanish army, establish the dogma. This view, however, prevailed before we had any knowledge of the twenty-odd universities in the Spanish Empire where men could get an education; it certainly cannot stand when we come upon the three or four schools now famous for their preparation of rebel leaders. Bolívar, Miranda, and San Martín, though they had no degrees themselves, are only three against 150,000 degree-holders graduating in the Spanish colonies. So dominant has been the idea that a really advanced outlook on philosophy, science, and politics could be picked up only in Europe that some Guatemalan writers have even tried to attribute the attainments of Flores and Goicoechea to European travel. These men, to be sure, did go abroad, but after, not before, they had been educated and had reached the peaks of their scientific careers and had made their contributions. Even they themselves were at first so much the victims of this provincial view that they were surprised to find when they reached Europe that they already knew most of what they encountered there and in some cases were disillusioned to find that they had gone on beyond the European celebrities.

By now it should be plain that one need not weep over the plight of the colonial student. The textbook writer will dwell scornfully upon the meagerness of his library and regale the innocent with descriptions of the

---

[7] ED. NOTE: Here Professor Lanning refers to a short poem used earlier in his work to indicate the eclectic spirit of Hispanic American savants in the eighteenth century. It runs as follows:

> Bad wine I decline,
> Good wine I find fine,
> And have no penchant
> To know if its modern or ancient.

sterile monotony of his classroom. Yet he had more books at his command than students in the United States fifty or seventy-five years ago had in institutions that now boast of their million-volume libraries. In Latin, he had a better grounding, defective as it was, than the current mass of our college men will ever have in living foreign languages. He had a grasp of basic terms and processes of reasoning that enabled him to shift from one intellectual climate to another with the ease that would make our twentieth-century undergraduate seem unlettered and immature. His command of political materials astounded foreigners who heard him debating the deep, complex issues of early independence.

Before taking a stand, the fastidious modern who feels that academic culture in the Spanish colonial city was "nauseatingly peripatetic" ought to assure himself, by making use of history and logic, that his delicate sensibilities will not be offended just as easily by university culture in a European city in the seventeenth and eighteenth centuries. He should be doubly sure that he is comparing American students with European students and not with overseas scientists and heroes at the peaks of thought and science. Once these tolerant precautions are taken—and who has ever noticed that they are?—he will see that as the eighteenth century advanced, questioning and experiment gained momentum everywhere. It is doubtful, however, whether he will be able to establish that academic life in Guatemala at any one time was inferior, for instance, to that of Italy which, in fact, was remarkably parallel in this respect to the Spanish Empire. He will find that the lag of American learning behind European, far from being "three hundred years," was probably never very great and that in the second half of the eighteenth century the gap closed so rapidly that only the time needed to cross the ocean remained.

OBSCURANTISM?

Spanish policy was not framed to prevent the spread of learning and wisdom. In fact, two trends of the age combined to give the Enlightenment special strength in America.

The zeal for "useful knowledge," the first of these, reached the Spanish colonies undiminished. Humboldt[8] noticed that in the Spanish Empire, "as in many parts of Europe, the sciences are thought to occupy the

---

[8] ED. NOTE: Baron Frederick Henry Alexander von Humboldt (1769-1859), a famous German scientist who visited America between 1799 and 1804, and who wrote a good deal concerning its physical environment, natural life, and economic, social, and political conditions.

mind only so far as they confer some immediate and practical benefit on society." The first great teacher of physics in the University of San Carlos de Guatemala justified his subject by "its very utility." The potential "use" of electricity in healing became an obsession there and provoked intense discussion and debate.

The extreme paternalism of the Spanish government, the other factor, was quick and efficient in the spread of useful knowledge and new discovery. It is hardly imaginable that the English government should spend on botanical research in the colonies, as the Madrid government did, a hundred times the annual budget of a respectable university. Through circulars telling how to perform the Caesarean operation, or describing highly effective new remedies for such afflictions as malaria, tetanus, and the dread jigger fleas, it protected the public with a zeal hardly equaled to the present day. The *protomedicato*, the branch of government responsible for the regulation of the medical profession, the protection of public health, and plant study, was unique among the institutions of colonizing powers in America. This ready-made mechanism, or the frame of mind that produced it, put Spain in the van of all European nations in vaccinating her people. The Economic Society existed upon the sufferance, if not upon the revenue, of the crown. Its mouthpiece the *Gazeta de Guatemala,* until it was overwhelmed trying to report the news of the Napoleonic wars, carried a description of every fragment of scientific information that could possibly be put to use. It went even beyond the scientific aims of the Enlightenment in an attempt to break the commercial isolation of Guatemala.

But, comes the hardy and perennial query, was the colonial scholar not cramped and dwarfed by the censorship of the Inquisition? Told of the horrors of the Holy Tribunal by every guide who has conducted him through the underground kitchens of a Spanish fort, the Anglo-Saxon can think of the Inquisition only as a kind of colonial Buchenwald. He must, nevertheless, understand that there was ample room for keeping up with the world without violating either canon or civil law. Few requests by scholars to read prohibited books were denied. And, besides, there were many perfectly legitimate links with the outside. The books most frequently denounced, those of Voltaire and Cadalso,[9] were more the classics of satire than the essentials of science, which crossed the frontiers in a hundred readily admitted works. Father Feijóo,[10] for example, digested all the new ideas and discoveries in the world of learning and,

[9] ED. NOTE: José Cadalso (1741-1782), a Spanish satiric writer.

[10] ED. NOTE: Fr. Benito Jerónimo Feijóo y Montenegro (1676-1764), a Spanish savant of the mid-eighteenth century, who pled for more empirical study; sometimes called the Spanish Voltaire.

in two different serial publications, got them over to many men who then as now would never have heard of them if they had had to wait to study the originals personally. The textbook in philosophy was exactly the same as the one considered ideal in the schools of France in 1788. It is doubtful if there was anybody in Europe better qualified than Theodoro d'Almeida to prepare the textbook on technical subjects used in Guatemala. The Inquisition, for that matter, became moribund and ineffective. Both the Roman and Madrid indexes of prohibited books were increasingly disregarded until the threat of revolution led the civil government, in some degree, to revitalize them.

It was just as difficult in a capital of the Spanish Empire as in John Milton's backyard to pound up crows by shutting the garden gate. Guatemala, like every such capital, had its circle of modern men who, broadcasting from brow to brow, violated the Index like an invisible network. Though the ratio of creoles to Spaniards among them was better than five to one,[11] there were in this coterie three Spanish judges of the "supreme court," one who had made the collection of prohibited books for the library of the University of Salamanca in Charles III's time, another who lent his prestige to the "economical society," notoriously a pool of the Enlightenment, and still another who could jest of Peripateticism as "a squid that gives off a black fluid to blind its pursuers." It was unthinkable that there should be an important idea abroad not the property of some of these men, whose very inspiration was a desire to "disseminate" whatever they had in mind—whether new ideas or improved seeds. Famous scientists from other capitals in the Empire, such as Mutis in Bogotá, sent in letters for publication. Members of the Spanish botanical expedition stimulated scholars by appearing in person. Conversation and the *Gazeta de Guatemala* carried the pollen from one group to another, thus blending the thought of the nation's intellectuals with that of the learned Spaniards having experience in other American capitals. Since the whole blend was inevitably dominated by members of the University cloister, the academic community gained a political influence in the late colonial period that has, somehow, remained characteristic of the university in that part of the world.

Baldly put, both the Inquisitorial and royal university censors did not aim to suppress enlightenment but to achieve it—by force, if necessary. In fact, the examiners (*calificadores*) of the Inquisition in the eighteenth century, like Diego Cisneros of Lima, were chosen because they were scholarly in temperament, eager to keep pace with a changing world and, perchance, to give it a little shove from behind now and then. Such a

[11] ED. NOTE: Here Professor Lanning makes the distinction between the creoles, whites born in the New World, and Spaniards, whites born in Spain.

man, though likely to be a friar or canon of a cathedral, was himself generally making a collection of prohibited books. On the wave, of prestige set in motion and rolled up by the reformers in the Aleas[12] affair, Dr. Goicoechea, who had a shelf of prohibited books in his cell, became examiner of the Inquisition in Guatemala. Among the important personalities denounced in the last phase of the Inquisition, Antonio Larrazábal was the most respected creole member of the cloister and the *oidor* Jacobo de Villa Urrutia, the outstanding Spaniard in the circle of the Economic Society. The censorship, then, was more an inconvenience than a social disgrace or an absolute barrier to ideas. The *censores regios,* a creation of Charles III, aimed not to mutilate and prevent the circulation of books in the Spanish world, but to get rid of sham in philosophy, bad taste in literature, and the dross of the ages in general, though not, of course, the dross of royal absolutism. The *Institutes* of Calvinism could hardly have been more "abhorred" nor more violently pounced upon than the annoying vestiges of overaged and empty formalism.

The reformers in San Carlos, the dominant element, were one with these academic censors in their scorn of the stale, hollow remnants of the "decadent Schoolmen." Both aimed to end pomposity, pretension, obscurity, and complexity. As a result, memorizing textbooks by rote—the gateway to learning without understanding—that in one generation could raise a boy of fourteen up to be a lawyer before the royal *audiencia,* had in the next fallen entirely from grace. Students went on strike against "dictation" in class. A group of doctors and licentiates proposed a system of selecting professors that could tax the minds rather than the memory of the competitors. Their leader, with his tongue in his cheek more often than behind his teeth, took the old Schoolmen's trick, approved in the University statutes, of opposing "contrary doctrines" one to the other in order to elbow aside an outmoded doctrine. Their hostility to another chair of theology, the "supreme faculty" of the "old" universities, was general and decisive. The same men urgently attacked Latin as the language of the University, not because they did not admire and wish to read classic literature, but because mouthing stereotyped phrases, held together by the shaky inflection of a few verbs and nouns, was an imposture. It was a sham, for Spanish, the vernacular and perfectly understood tongue, was clandestinely used in class. Latin was pretentious and disgusting when shallow men used it as a jargon to impress the

---

[12] ED. NOTE: A Spanish Dominican, Fermín Aleas, came to Guatemala after the earthquake of 1773 and made reckless charges against the University, forcing an investigation by the cloister.

humble man and as a cloak to conceal their ignorance from him. The objection to the chair of Cakchiquel[13] was not that the language was dead but that the chair was a fake. To tie up the salary needed for another chair for 140 years in order to keep up appearances without teaching the language was precisely the kind of folly and dishonesty the anti-Peripatetic detested.

WHAT DID RETARD ACADEMIC CULTURE?

If the colonies were not intellectually isolated and the policy of the mother country was not obscurantist, what then did prevent the healthiest possible growth of academic culture in Guatemala? It was not want of ideas, not lack of energy, not even the baneful eye of the censor clutching the ever-celebrated *Index Librorum Prohibitorum* in his griffin claws, but in the cold language of the Spanish bookkeeper, pesos, reales, maravedis—in short, money.

A contracting economy, pinched to begin with, was eventually so straitened by the blockade in a series of wars, begun by the revolt of the English mainland colonies and continued in the Napoleonic struggles, that the market collapsed. Indigo plantations dropped 70 or 80 per cent in value, and corporations, incessantly called upon for donations to support such foreign entanglements as the American Revolution, struggled, sometimes in vain, to hold onto the appropriation they had had since the seventeenth century. Upon retiring, proprietary professors, as the law entitled them to do, held on to most of their salaries and made the profession of learning even less remunerative than it is by nature and, in consequence, less attractive to young men. One persistent professor taught a much needed chair of law without salary for seventeen years.

Intellectuals were thus harried by commercial and financial, but not by literary or scientific, isolation. A half-adequate university income, not to mention an expanding economy such as Havana had enjoyed since the British occupation of 1762, would have made the difference between a struggling educational life and a flourishing one. The cloister of the University of San Carlos, pathetically eager for a chair of mathematics, learned from businessmen at home and the auditor's office in Madrid that money alone stood between them and chairs in anatomy, surgery, experimental physics, botany, Oriental languages, and other humanistic studies. Petty little devices to raise funds for current books, a proud professor working with his own hands or investing his own money to

[13] ED. NOTE: The Guatemalan Indian language.

provide laboratory instruments, show better than any disquisition where the true handicaps really were. The plan to bring in students from all the capitals in Central America on fellowships, train them, and return them to provide medical care fell through because the provinces had nothing left to tax for the purpose. The general schemes to give rudimentary, but scientific, medical and surgical instruction to young men and obstetrical training to midwives from the villages, who would otherwise end up as medicine men and *curanderas,* came to nothing for the same reason. The leading professors of medicine—Flores, Esparragosa, Molina, Larrave— all recognized the tragic deficiency of medical education.

Yet, like Omar Khayyám, we come out the door wherein we went: that of money. Poor returns for the exertions of a well-trained doctor and inadequate funds for the establishment and well-rounded operations of schools of medicine and surgery left the multitudes to their misery or to their own pathetic means. The whole cloister was so aware of its problems, so attuned to the times, that it advised against another chair of theology and recommended the liquidation of the ineffective chair of Indian language to save money. Beyond money, however progressive the crown might be, there were political obstructions developing in direct ratio to progress in learning.

For one thing, paternalism, though it facilitated the modern scientific drift, operated in reverse in any particular touching the prerogatives of the crown. By 1785, the guild charters and exemptions, upon which the very existence of the universities originally depended, were in full decline before the remorseless pressure of the regalist lawyers. The medieval autonomy of the cloister had made Salamanca the scene of a prolonged fight when Charles III tried to turn it into a subordinate block on the pyramid of reconstruction. In Guatemala the royal vice closed inexorably upon the academic franchises inherited from this same university.

The autonomy of the University, as if it had been a man, writhed before it was quiet. When San Carlos combined the arms of the Pope with those of the king on the façade of its building, the crown officers had them chiseled out. They sneered at the move to appoint a "university fiscal" in the case, though this was permissible under the statutes of the University, as if only old and hopeless Peripatetics could "nowadays" be so simple as to put any stock in those old charters. In the same mood, the Superior Government, in violation of both the customs and laws of San Carlos, substituted the regent of the *audiencia* for the captain general in doctoral investitures to lessen the prestige of the cloister.

Such hampering interposition was now common. No artistic, literary, or intellectual choice was too sacred nor anything too trifling for the crown to decide, especially if it permitted the king to intrude himself in a matter the cloister might once have decided for itself. Permission for Dr. Esparragosa to wear the new uniform of an Honorary Surgeon of H. M.'s Bedchamber to the cloister meetings, though only University customs could possibly be violated, was decided by the crown. The great "guild" that was the University was reduced to impotence when, on the eve of independence, the most famous and beloved member of the cloister was arrested in Spain and thrown into prison. The *protomedicato,* an old Castilian institution ideally suited to the protection of the public health, and more up to date in the handling of cases of malpractice in medicine than anything we have today, likewise fell a victim to regalism. Before Napoleon had touched off rebellion in the colonies, that tribunal had had all its vital powers shaken from it and, so it is learned, instead of prosecuting and trying charlatans, could content itself in the future with offering the civil authorities harmless professional opinions. Thus the University and the *protomedicato,* the two institutions where medieval autonomy blended so naturally with the hope of progress in modern times, at the last moment went limp in the tightening hold of regalism.

There is also, after all, a certain truth in the claim that the "vestiges of formalism" did in some degree slow down the progress of learning in the kingdom. Those "remnants" would not have enraged the reformers as they did had they not been realities and personalities taking "an unconscionable time adying." Some mildly complained in 1782 that, as one of them put it, they "had suffered at the hands of the Peripatetics." The few die-hards did not have the strength to achieve this delay alone, though the minority in the cloister fighting against change had a powerful but unwitting ally in the nature of the human race. They had another in the childishly intransigent Dominicans in the City who, like Luis de Escoto, were no whit superior to the small clump of Dominican religious in Bogotá who wanted to debate Copernicus "pro and con" as late as 1774. Newton meant little more to these men than the champion Chinese kiteflyer. One of them, Fray José Arce, went to the length of reporting Goicoechea for political "propositions" and for having prohibited books in his cell, and certain other rival Franciscans for moral peccadillos. As an army not committed to battle is "a force in being" neutralizing an equal enemy force, so the censorship of the Inquisition, whatever protection it might have afforded morality, religion, or authority, was always "an evil in being" capable of canceling out an equal amount of good. Or so the Anglo-American is likely to feel, yet there have been times in the last ten years when buying certain books or showing too much familiarity with them could be more dangerous to the good name of an American public figure than was the holding of prohibited books in colonial Guatemala.

SAN CARLOS AND REVOLUTION

Within the scholastic framework the Guatemalan student prepared himself for the epoch of independence. Inadequate though the subject was, he found room, while treating ethics—"a branch of statecraft"—to ponder the question of the basis of sovereignty derived from the people. The doctrine of popular sovereignty had been upheld by such famous church writers as Suárez and Bellarmine. In a situation like that prevailing in America after the dethronement of Ferdinand VII in 1808, a student could utter "popular sovereignty" with exterior innocence while directing all minds to the watchwords of the American and French revolutions. The two most conspicuous student defenders of this "stale scholastic" doctrine of popular sovereignty, Manuel Antonio de Molina and Marcial Zebadúa, became precursors of independence. Thus, although the University was not a focus of revolution, much less a "cell" of conspiracy, it could and did offer familiarity with the world of ideas. The host of men that gathered after independence to debate the form of government of the new states with an erudition that ranged over the whole course of history had something they did not pick up on the trip to the convention hall.

Guatemala, too, had its rebirth of social consciousness before independence, and in this movement prominent university figures like José Antonio Goicoechea and Matías de Córdoba took most conspicuous part. To be sure, Simón Bergaño y Villegas, who spoke of making nobility by the sweat of the other man's brow, went beyond any academic person in public discussion and clearly set the socially conscious off from the provincial aristocracy which, with few exceptions, was one with the University cloister.

Thus in the Kingdom of Guatemala literate people understood the doctrine of popular sovereignty and knew that their social system, whether it could be remedied or not, was inequitable. But these two views were very advanced and only a few people—mostly those like Pedro Molina, the illegitimate, and Simón Bergaño, the obscure, who did not qualify for the aristocracy—embraced them. In addition to this small group of radicals, elbowed out of the picture until the last moment, there were two other groups—the provincial aristocracy and the Peninsular Spaniards. These two had much in common. The creole aristocrats infiltrated the court in the last two decades before independence and were as much tied up with office-holding under Spain as were the Spaniards. Old Captain General Carlos de Urrutia was himself Cuban creole; the *auditor de guerra,* José Cecilio del Valle, was a progressive Central American. The Ayzinenas offer a perfect example of the difficulty many in Guatemala felt when the Empire began to disintegrate. Having gained wealth in business enterprises and recognition of social prestige in a title of nobility, the family could place Dr. José in Madrid as counselor of state in the last years of the colonial period.

Not only did these provincial aristocrats look with nostalgia upon bygone days, but they mortally feared an uprising of the inarticulate and, in the main, leaderless Indians. And well might they tremble, for, at the first tidings of the declaration of independence, the rowdies of Alma- chapán castrated the "overseas" white men in town. Responsible Indians like the Cacique Presbyter José Tomás Ruiz, who were university gradu- ates and capable of leading the native mass on a class or racial footing, preferred to regard themselves socially as creoles and to join the con- spirators of Belén, who depended upon a palace uprising and not upon mob action of their people. Servile insurrection made no appeal to them. All of this made the well-to-do cling to the possibility of continuing the status quo—precarious though it became—which the Spanish party rep- resented. This is not to say that the creoles did not have any spirit of local patriotism, for José del Valle who headed the "Bacos"—the party of the status quo—made a strong case for eventual independence in the "extraordinary session" of the *ayuntamiento* of Guatemala that broke forever the bonds with the mother country. It was an Ayzinena—Don Mariano—who suggested this session to Gainza. After Iturbide's *coup d'état,* when it was no longer possible to depend upon the broken reed of Spanish power, the creoles joined the two or three extremists and turned to independence. Nothing had changed in Guatemala—only events had taken place outside Guatemala which the leaders there were obliged to take into account. Just as formerly it behooved the creoles to stick with the Spaniards, the Spaniards now must needs go along with the creoles. That Gainza salvaged and continued his very office is proof that the maneuvers had succeeded on both sides. It should come, therefore, as no surprise that these two factions favored monarchy as the best means of preventing a social upheaval that might dethrone them as well as the king of Spain.

In any terms, save those of patriotism, independence was a worse disaster to the University of San Carlos than the earthquake of 1773. In the decade before the great earthquake, San Carlos conferred 122 bache- lors' and 30 higher degrees, while, in the succeeding ten years, it awarded 119 bachelors' and 42 higher degrees. The decade from 1812 to 1821 produced 375 bachelors' degrees and 40 superior degrees for an annual average of 41.5 degrees a year, while, in contrast, during the first years of independence (1822-1829) only 117 bachelors' and 7 higher degrees could be awarded. This was an average of only 15.5 degrees a year, or a little more than one-third of the showing of the previous decade.

Neither did independence produce an intellectual revolution, for the great steps forward in this area had been taken in the previous generation and a half. Much of the old formalism and certainty, whether philosophical or financial, had been temporarily lost and a dry decadence and purposelessness took over in the University. How imperfectly the anarchy of the early national period and the rigid social stratification of the colonial yielded to the need for fundamental reformation is the proper subject for another book.

Science and Observation in Eighteenth-Century English America

LOUIS B. WRIGHT

In this selection, Louis B. Wright, long-time director of the Folger Library, demonstrates that in the eighteenth century the thirteen English colonies, like those in Spanish America, were alive with the new ideas of the Scientific Revolution and the empiricism and experimentation it brought with it. Above all Benjamin Franklin stood out as the representative of eighteenth-century American science with his theoretical and experimental investigations of electricity, heat, and other subjects; his pleas for useful knowledge; and his organization of the American Philosophical Society. But Franklin's towering figure must not be allowed to obscure the host of other, less familiar figures who made significant contributions to the advancement of learning.

On the whole both Lanning and Wright show the similarities in the scientific

Pp. 223-237 in *The Cultural Life of the American Colonies, 1607-1763* by Louis B. Wright. Copyright © 1957 by Harper & Row, Publishers, Incorporated. Used by permission of the publishers.

movements and intellectual life in Spanish and British America. If there was a difference in either degree or direction, Lanning stresses the activities of a university faculty while Wright, though he does not deny the importance of work at Harvard and Yale, emphasizes the contributions of individuals outside an institutional setting. From this divergence could it be argued that the spirit of inquiry was more widespread in English America—or is this but one more example of the prejudices and prejudgments to which we are all prone and which comparative study will put to stern tests?

SCIENTIFIC INTEREST INCREASED AND MATURED AS THE SEVENTEENTH century drew to a close, and by the early years of the eighteenth century the colonies had a respectable number of "philosophers" —as scientists were then described—who could discourse learnedly about physics, chemistry, astronomy, medicine, and related subjects. An ancient heresy that the Puritans were opposed to experimental science generally is not borne out by the facts. The Puritans, it is true, sought to demonstrate the handiwork of God in the wonders of nature, but they were not alone in this endeavor. William Byrd, for example, in his tract on the plague devoted considerable effort to showing the manifestation of God's will in the visitations of pestilence. The Puritans proved receptive to both Copernican astronomy and Newtonian physics. A suggestion that Puritans favored Copernican astronomy partly because they believed Catholics opposed it is found in a statement by Charles Morton accepting Galileo's confirmation of the new theories. "Only Papists were tender of declaring their mind too plainly in this matter," Morton asserted, "because the Pope (forsooth out of a private peck to Galilaeus) had from St. Peter's Chair condemned the opinion." In Newton's assertion of the laws of nature, Puritans discovered proof of God's revelation of His immutable laws. Although some did not miss the mechanistic and materialistic implications of Newton, which were to disturb religious ideas throughout the century, Puritan casuistry enabled men like Cotton Mather, and later Jonathan Edwards, to turn Newton to their own philosophic purposes.

During the first decades of the eighteenth century, American colleges began to pay more attention to scientific subjects. The first chair of science in an American college was established at the College of William and Mary in 1711 with the appointment of a certain Mr. LeFevre as professor of natural philosophy and mathematics. Unhappily LeFevre did little to advance knowledge because he soon fell victim to "an idle hussy" and strong drink, twin hazards which an academic man even in tolerant Williamsburg could not survive. Six years later William and

Mary appointed the Reverend Hugh Jones, a man of probity, to teach courses in mathematics and natural philosophy. Since the students at William and Mary, the sons of Virginia planters, were directly concerned with the application of mathematics and scientific knowledge to the problems of existence, Jones emphasized arithmetic, algebra, geometry, surveying, and navigation.

A genuine advance in scientific instruction resulted from the establishment at Harvard in 1727 of an endowed chair of mathematics and natural philosophy through the generosity of Thomas Hollis of London. The first incumbent of the Hollis professorship was Isaac Greenwood, a Harvard graduate, who had gone to England to study divinity but wound up listening to lectures on mathematics and physics by disciples of Newton. Greenwood introduced new courses in mathematics at Harvard, published a textbook in arithmetic, and prepared a manuscript text in algebra. He also gave his students an indoctrination in Newtonian physics. But like LeFevre at William and Mary, Greenwood too was overtaken in drink and dismissed from his professorship.

Greenwood's successor was John Winthrop IV, who held the Hollis professorship from 1738 until his death in 1779. His course in natural philosophy provided the most advanced scientific instruction in North America in its time, and Winthrop was honored for his learning. One of his first steps after receiving the appointment was to procure a copy of Newton's *Principia,* which became his guide. Friends in England sent Winthrop books and "philosophical apparatus," including a telescope which had belonged to Edmund Halley, after whom a spectacular comet was named. Said to have been the first in America to teach Newton's fluxions (calculus), Winthrop stimulated a fresh interest in mathematics, theoretical speculation, and investigation. He gave an impetus to theoretical studies, or what today we would call "pure science," as distinguished from the mere practical application of knowledge. His astronomical observations attracted widespread attention. During his long career he published six pamphlets and contributed eleven papers to the Royal Society. In recognition of his scientific contributions the University of Edinburgh conferred upon him the honorary degree of doctor of laws. With the progress made by Winthrop at Harvard academic training in science came of age in this country.

Other institutions made slower progress. Yale, more conservative than Harvard, held on to Aristotelian theories until well into the eighteenth century. An intellectual explosion, however, was set off by the arrival in New Haven of a shipment of books collected in England by Jeremiah Dummer, who had persuaded Newton, Halley, and other distinguished members of the Royal Society to contribute some of their own works.

From these books students and faculty alike gained a new vision of science and speculative philosophy. One of those affected was Samuel Johnson, later to be president of King's College (Columbia), a member of the class of 1714. Between 1716 and 1719, Johnson, a tutor at Yale, undertook to revise mathematical instruction and introduced the study of algebra. From this time forward, scientific instruction improved at Yale. One may also conjecture that the reading of Dummer's books helped persuade Johnson and others of his college generation to join the Anglican Church, an event that vastly disturbed Yale's orthodox Congregationalists.

Scientific speculation and experiment, however, were not such an exclusive academic monopoly in the seventeenth and eighteenth centuries as they are in our age. Individuals throughout the colonies developed their special interests, ordered books and apparatus from London, and communicated with like-minded people. Urban centers naturally offered the best opportunities for scientific discussion and the meeting of kindred spirits. Boston, Newport, New York, Philadelphia, and Charleston, South Carolina, were notable for the scientific interests of some of their citizens. At the turn of the century, the Cambridge-Boston region had a greater concentration of natural philosophers than any other part of the country, but by 1750 Philadelphia had taken the lead.

The concentration of learned clergymen in New England helps to explain the early and widespread interest in science in that region, for the clergy adapted science to their own pious purposes, not always realizing where their investigations might ultimately lead them. The most advanced scientific thinker among them was probably Cotton Mather, son of Increase Mather, who also displayed keen interest in natural phenomena. Cotton Mather, for all his learning, exhibited a curious mixture of rationalism and superstitious credulity, as evidenced in his espousal of the witchcraft delusion in 1692.

The impact of the new science had produced a number of treatises in England by pious natural philosophers who sought to prove that science could be the handmaiden of religion. Robert Boyle's *Usefulness of Experimental Natural Philosophy* (1663) was typical of the school of natural theology, to which Cotton Mather in 1720 contributed *The Christian Philosopher,* a tract summarizing his own scientific beliefs and setting forth the thesis that science was an incentive to rather than an enemy of religion.

Mather sent to the Royal Society a manuscript containing observations on rainbows, rattlesnakes, plants, and variations in the magnetic needle, along with a letter hinting that he would welcome election. So impressed were the members with his data that they elected him a fellow in 1713, and Mather characteristically became one of their most prolific contributors.

He also advanced his own scientific thinking by reading the papers of the Royal Society. Two months after publication of reports on the success of inoculation for smallpox, Mather was advocating the new technique in the Boston epidemic of 1721. Convinced by Mather's evidence, Dr. Zabdiel Boylston successfully inoculated his own son and two Negro servants. Although nearly three hundred Bostonians received inoculation during the year and only six died, the public outcry against Mather and Boylston was excessive and resulted in attempts at bodily violence. Nevertheless they stood their ground and continued to recommend and practice inoculation as a method of combating one of the terrifying diseases of the day. Although the controversy that started in Boston broke out in other localities throughout the colonies where inoculation was tried, time eventually justified Mather's enlightened views.

If Cotton Mather was the most learned of the New Englanders, others were only a little behind him. Thomas Brattle, a wealthy Boston merchant, made such careful observations of Halley's comet in 1680 that Newton cited his data in the *Principia*. During the witchcraft hysteria at Salem, Brattle displayed an enlightened point of view, in contrast to Mather's; his reasoned and calm plea for justice to the accused persons had the urbanity and rational approach characteristic of a scientific mind in the next century. Brattle's brother William was elected to the Royal Society in 1713. Paul Dudley, a lawyer, sent to the Royal Society papers on a variety of subjects including the preparation of maple sugar; plant breeding of pumpkins, Indian corn, and squash; the habits and value of whales; and an account of New England's earthquakes, including the most recent, which occurred on October 29, 1727. In the latter paper Dudley explained the rhythmic motion of the earthquake as movements in the earth's crust—a far cry from the less enlightened notion that it merely represented God's angry shaking up of sinners. About a quarter of a century later Professor John Winthrop of Harvard further advanced thinking on the subject of earthquakes by comparing the waves of motion in the earth to musical vibrations.

During the first half of the eighteenth century, the rapid growth of Philadelphia, its broad tolerance, and the diversity of its citizens' background gave that city an intellectual vitality not equaled elsewhere in the colonies. James Logan, whose own interests in mathematics and physics had led him to import some of the latest books on these subjects, including Newton's *Principia,* opened his library to any intelligent reader and encouraged talented young men to pursue mathematical and scientific studies. Such an atmosphere was conducive to the development of a spirit of free inquiry, and it was no accident that a group of alert craftsmen under the leadership of Benjamin Franklin should establish in 1727 a society called the Junto whose purpose was discussion and intellectual stimulation. As Philadelphia grew into the greatest port in the colonies, its commercial ties with the outer world increased and the contacts of its merchants with businessmen abroad helped to open channels for the communication of ideas.

One of the most important of these intellectual intermediaries was Peter Collinson, a London merchant, who had been brought up a Quaker. Himself a member of the Royal Society and keenly interested in natural philosophy, Collinson served as agent for English virtuosos who wanted specimens from the New World. Through his business connections, he established contacts with American collectors and observers and assisted them in procuring books, materials, and instruments. About 1730, through the good offices of Joseph Breintnal, one of Franklin's Junto, Collinson learned about a promising young naturalist, John Bartram, a Philadelphia Quaker, who had been inspired to pursue botanical studies by James Logan, a botanist of some attainments himself. Collinson's correspondence with Bartram, which lasted until the former's death in 1768, proved mutually helpful. The extant letters provide an insight into the curiosity of Europeans about American natural history and the devotion of men like Bartram to the study of the world about them. Collinson, the Duke of Richmond, and Lord Petre each subscribed ten guineas a year for specimens which Bartram collected and sent them. In 1765 George III appointed Bartram botanist to the King at fifty pounds per year; the royal horticultural gardens were soon filled with plants, shrubs, and trees sent over by the indefatigable Quaker, who traveled at various times from the Great Lakes to Florida on collecting expeditions.

The letters exchanged between Collinson and Bartram are filled with acute scientific observations, as well as much of human interest. On one occasion Collinson urges his Quaker friend to be neat and careful of his dress on a journey into Virginia "and not appear to disgrace thyself or me; for . . . these Virginians are a very gentle, well-dressed people, and look, perhaps, more at a man's outside than his inside." On another occasion Collinson banteringly reproves Bartram for having given away an old cap which he had sent him because it had a hole or two in it. At least the lining was new, and if Bartram had returned it, it would have "served me two or three years, to have worn in the country, in rainy weather."

Bartram established a botanical garden on the Schuylkill River three miles from Philadelphia where he could cultivate and study specimens collected on his journeys. Scholarly in his approach, he learned Latin in order to read the works of the Swedish scientist, Linnaeus, the greatest botanist of the age. The fame of Bartram's knowledge of botany and other phases of natural history spread abroad. His reports to Collinson, his journals, and the specimens which he sent to Europe made his name familiar in scientific circles everywhere. Linnaeus called him the greatest contemporary "natural botanist" and sent his favorite student, Peter Kalm, to visit his garden and talk with him. Franklin had great respect for his knowledge and transmitted to Jefferson a suggestion made by Bartram for exploring the western portion of the continent, a suggestion that may have influenced Jefferson's plans for the Lewis and Clark expedition. Bartram's son William followed in his father's footsteps and became a naturalist of some note.

Bartram and his garden near Philadelphia served as a focus for a great deal of American interest in botany and related subjects. Most of the American naturalists were in communication with him, and he supplied them with information as well as materials.

Of all the colonial naturalists, Bartram is best remembered today, but others were not far behind him in contemporary fame. John Banister, of Charles City County, Virginia, an Anglican parson by profession, devoted himself to botany, zoology, and entomology, but his career was cut short in 1692 when a companion on an expedition to the Roanoke River accidentally shot him. He was in communication with John Ray, the English botanist, and supplied Ray and others with accurate descriptions of Virginia plants and animals. John Clayton, who was appointed attorney general for Virginia in 1705, planted a botanical garden and spent much time in the collection and study of plants. Specimens, drawings, and information which he supplied enabled John Frederick Gronovius of Leiden to prepare his *Flora Virginica* (1739-1743). Dr. John Mitchell, of Urbanna, Virginia, fellow of the Royal Society, wrote on botany, zoology, and medicine; he corresponded with Linnaeus, Gronovius, Collinson, and other Europeans interested in natural history. Dr. Cadwallader Colden, physician, merchant, scientist, and finally lieutenant governor of New York, supplied Linnaeus with descriptions of the flora of New York for publication in the transactions of the Royal Society of Upsala. His broad scientific interests also included medicine, mathematics, physics, and anthropology. Colden wrote on yellow fever, cancer, the "throat distemper" (diphtheria), the virtues of tar water, light, color, gravitation, and a variety of other topics, including *The History of the Five Indian Nations,* first published in 1727.

The career of Dr. Alexander Garden of Charleston, South Carolina, who gave his name to the gardenia, illustrates the community of interest of these eighteenth-century naturalists. A Scottish physician who settled in South Carolina shortly after he received a medical degree from Aberdeen in 1753, Garden was soon avidly studying the natural history of his adopted country. On a visit to New York in 1754 he met Cadwallader Colden and saw in his library some of the latest works of Linnaeus. On the journey south from New York he visited John Bartram in Philadelphia and began a correspondence with Colden, Bartram, and John Clayton of Virginia. Soon he was also corresponding with the leading naturalists of Europe: Linnaeus, Gronovius, Collinson, and others. In 1763 he was elected a member of the Royal Society of Upsala and ten years later a fellow of the Royal Society of London. A Tory at the onset of the Revolution, he left South Carolina to die in London. Garden's observations of plants and animals were unusually accurate and many of his deductions were scientifically ahead of his time.

The community of interest displayed by the naturalists is indicative of the intellectual climate that induced Benjamin Franklin to propose in 1743 the establishment of the American Philosophical Society. Franklin had already been in communication with scientists throughout the colonies. Well acquainted with Bartram and his group, he had also been in correspondence with Collinson and other scientists in England and on the Continent. From his own experience and his knowledge of the amount of scientific interest dispersed through the colonies, Franklin realized that a society where information could be pooled and ideas exchanged would have immense benefits for the whole country. As he conceived his plan, the Society, centered in Philadelphia, would devote itself to the "promotion of useful knowledge." Although it was primarily designed to be utilitarian, mathematics and the more abstract sciences would have a place. Franklin thought that the Society could best serve mankind by collecting data on useful plants, animals, and minerals and by encouraging needed inventions. Kindred spirits agreed with Franklin, and by 1744 he had organized the American Philosophical Society with himself as secretary. Franklin was disappointed because some of the members were "very idle gentlemen," but in 1769 the Philosophical Society united with the American Society, which had grown out of Franklin's old Junto, and henceforth became a more active and mature scientific organization.

On a trip to Boston in 1746, Franklin met a visiting Scot named Dr. Spence who had recently brought over an "electrical bottle," an early type of condenser, soon to be known as a Leyden jar. Excited by Spence's demonstrations, Franklin returned to Philadelphia and devoted himself with such zeal to electrical studies that within a few years he was known throughout the world as the first scientist in the American colonies.

Franklin set up a laboratory in his house and made improvements in the condensers and crude batteries then known. Retiring from his printing business in 1748, he now had leisure for study and experimentation which he turned to good advantage. He soon came to the conclusion that electricity generated in the laboratory and lightning from the clouds had the same properties. His letters to Collinson on the subject attracted the attention of other members of the Royal Society. In one of these letters, which Collinson had printed in the *Gentleman's Magazine* for May, 1750, Franklin characteristically made a suggestion for the practical application of the knowledge that he had accumulated through experimentation. This letter first suggested the use of lightning rods.

Other letters to Collinson detailed Franklin's views on the identity of electricity and lightning, a proposed method of testing this theory, and observations made in his various experiments. These Collinson had printed in London in 1751 as *Experiments and Observations on Electricity, Made at Philadelphia in America, by Mr. Benjamin Franklin*. A reprint of this volume with additions came out in 1753 and again in 1760-62. It was translated almost immediately into French, and later into German and Italian. Franklin found himself famous overnight. Honors came fast. Harvard, Yale, and William and Mary made him honorary Master of Arts. The Royal Society awarded him the Copley Medal. In 1759 the University of St. Andrews conferred upon him the degree of doctor of laws and henceforth he was known as "Dr. Franklin," a title that pleased him immensely. In 1762 Oxford gave him the degree of doctor of civil law.

The test of Franklin's proposed method of drawing electricity from a cloud was first made in France, and Franklin himself in the summer of 1752 made his famous experiment with the kite. Throughout the learned world, the excitement over electricity spread Franklin's fame. Many repeated his experiments, and at least one scientist, a Swede, lost his life drawing lightning from the clouds by Franklin's methods. In the meantime, Franklin himself was busy persuading his fellow citizens that his studies would prove useful to any who cared to protect their houses and barns by the erection of lightning rods.

Electricity was not Franklin's only scientific interest. Throughout the rest of his life, even in the midst of political activity of great importance, he never forgot his "philosophical" studies, which included subjects as various as the habits of ants, the organisms in sea water, wind currents, eclipses, the causes of storm, and a hundred other matters which stirred his fertile imagination. A biographer appraising Franklin's experiments has observed that his contribution resulted from "a fundamental mind, which almost at once mastered the general problem as it then existed and went deeper into it than any observer had yet gone. He found electricity a curiosity and left it a science." Although Franklin got amusement and entertainment out of his scientific studies, his activities went beyond the sort of thing relished by the virtuosos to something that we can dignify as scientific thinking. Always he expressed himself with admirable clarity, precision, and a disdain of learned humbuggery. "If my hypothesis is not the truth," he observed of himself, "it is at least as naked. For I have not with some of our learned moderns disguised my nonsense in Greek, clothed it in algebra, or adorned it with fluxions. You have it *in purus naturalibus*."

Benjamin Franklin was not the only one of Philadelphia's craftsmen who acquired skill in scientific matters. Thomas Godfrey, a glazier and one of the original Junto, was befriended by his employer, James Logan, who encouraged him in mathematical and astronomical studies. Although Godfrey had little education, he showed a natural genius for these subjects. His chief accomplishment was the invention in 1730 of an improved mariner's quadrant for the determination of latitude. This is the quadrant named after John Hadley, who perfected one about the same time, possibly after hearing about Godfrey's instrument.

More distinguished than Godfrey was David Rittenhouse, a Philadelphia clock and instrument maker, who became an astronomer and mathematician of distinction. He was also interested in optics and in 1756 constructed a telescope which excited the admiration of his contemporaries. In 1767 he built an orrery—an instrument to show the relations of the various bodies in the solar system—which caused Jefferson to comment that he had approached nearer to the Almighty "than any man who has lived from the creation to this day." Rittenhouse's instruments as well as his theoretical knowledge helped to advance physical sciences and astronomy in the colonies and later in the new nation.

A combination of the practical and the theoretical characterized most scientific thinking in America in the eighteenth century. Jared Eliot of Connecticut was typical of his generation. Clergyman and physician, he also interested himself in experimental agriculture and mineralogy. His *Essay on Field Husbandry in New England,* published in six parts from 1748-1759, had considerable influence on farming. He and Ezra Stiles, later president of Yale, who also had many scientific interests, attempted to introduce silk culture in Connecticut. Eliot's *Essay on the Invention, or Art of Making Very Good, If Not the Best Iron, from Black Sea Sand* (1762) won a medal from the Royal Society. That Eliot was not merely a theoretician and a projector may be indicated by his own prosperity, which enabled him to endow a book fund at Yale.

Although colonial colleges gradually increased their emphasis on mathematics and natural philosophy as the eighteenth century wore on, scientific progress continued to center in nonacademic groups and in individuals like Bartram, Franklin, and Rittenhouse. Preachers, physicians, and lawyers as the most learned of society showed the greatest proficiency in scientific knowledge. From the mid-eighteenth century onward nearly every town of consequence had a few natural philosophers capable of performing an experiment with a Leyden jar, classifying the flora of the neighborhood according to Linnaeus, or giving an opinion on the cause of earthquakes or epidemics.

The vogue of natural philosophy was such that preachers even in their pulpits sometimes expounded God's wonders in the manner of a professor. Dr. Alexander Hamilton, physician of Annapolis, on a visit to Boston in July, 1744, found such a sermon at King's Chapel an annoyance. "He [the minister] gave us rather a philosophical lecture than a sermon . . ." Hamilton observes. "We had a load of impertinence from him about the specific gravity of air and water, the exhalation of vapours, the expansion and condensation of clouds, the operation of distillation, and the chemistry of nature. In fine it was but a very puerile physical lecture and no sermon at all." In the same year an anonymous poet published an "Epistle from Cambridge" in *The American Magazine and Historical Chronicle* lamenting that poets had been superseded in college by science:

> Now algebra, geometry,
> Arithmetic, astronomy,
> Optics, chronology, and statics,
> All tiresome parts of mathematics,
> With twenty harder names than these
> Disturb my brains, and break my peace.
> We're told how planets roll on high,
> How large their orbits, and how nigh;
> I hope in little time to know,
> Whether the moon's a cheese, or no.

Itinerant lecturers with a few pieces of philosophical apparatus went up and down the land explaining their marvels to open-mouthed audiences. The day of popular science had dawned, and the interest in natural wonders would increase from that time until our own.

Physicians occupied an increasingly important place in the scientific advances of the eighteenth century. Philadelphia developed a distinguished group of doctors interested in medical research. Partly as a result of the humanitarianism of the Quakers, partly because of the intelligence of a group of physicians, the first modern hospital in the North American colonies was erected in Philadelphia in 1755. This hospital attracted medical students and served as a training school until the opening of the school of medicine at the College of Philadelphia (later the University of Pennsylvania) in 1765.

The new medical school got off to a good start under the direction of two Philadelphians who had received their medical degrees at the University of Edinburgh, Dr. John Morgan and Dr. William Shippen. A part of the commencement exercises at the College of Philadelphia in May, 1765, was *A Discourse Upon the Institution of Medical Schools in America* delivered by Dr. Morgan. This address paved the way for the establishment of the school. That fall the college announced lectures in anatomy and surgery by Dr. Shippen and lectures in materia medica by Dr. Morgan. The first class of physicians graduated in 1768. The next year Dr. Benjamin Rush became professor of chemistry. The first medical school in North America was launched on a career destined to be long and distinguished. Three years after the medical school opened in Philadelphia, King's College (later Columbia) established a medical school with six of the ablest physicians in New York as a faculty.

Medical instruction helped to disseminate scientific knowledge, not merely among the profession, but among laymen as well, for lectures and demonstrations were frequently open to the public—for a fee. Dr. Shippen, for example, sold tickets to his lectures in anatomy at five shillings per meeting and did his best to enlist popular interest in education. Other physicians also welcomed lay auditors. Medical knowledge was regarded as a desirable addition to any eighteenth-century gentleman's training.

The zeal for lectures on all phases of natural philosophy increased as its wonders became more widely known. One of the most active lecturers was Ebenezer Kinnersley, a Pennsylvania Baptist preacher, who set out early in the 1750's to popularize Franklin's experiments in electricity. For the next thirty years Kinnersley lectured so constantly in various cities that in the popular consciousness he became a scientist better known than Franklin himself. During the 1760's and seventies in Philadelphia, lectures on popular science excited almost as much interest as the growing political controversies.

The reorganization in 1769 of the American Philosophical Society Held at Philadelphia for Promoting Useful Knowledge gave that body an intercolonial status and increased the scope of its activities. In that year the *American Magazine or General Repository* published serially some of the Society's most important papers. The reception of the learned contributions was so encouraging that in 1771 the Society began publishing its *Transactions*. These papers attracted attention among learned men throughout the colonies and won the acclaim of European scientists.

Rittenhouse's report on the transit of Venus was singled out for particular praise for the accuracy of its observations.

As the political controversies with the mother country multiplied, the need for improving scientific knowledge and applying technological skills became even more apparent. As always, war would create necessities that would have to be met by the best scientific talent available. The foundation for self-sustaining technological developments had already been laid in the broad scientific interests of the American people. As the membership of the American Philosophical Society illustrated, scientific knowledge and skill were not confined to any group or class. Aristocrats, farmers, craftsmen, and artisans of all kinds shared the secrets of natural philosophy.

SELECTED BIBLIOGRAPHY

Included in this bibliography is only a smattering of the basic English language titles useful for the student of comparative colonial history. The field is a vast one, and the works listed here can serve only as an introduction to the literature.

GENERAL WORKS

Lewis Hanke, ed., *Do the Americas Have a Common History?* (1963) is a discussion of the Bolton thesis, pro and con, on the unity of American history. Max Savelle's abridgement of Silvio Zavala's, *The Colonial Period in the History of the New World* (1961) makes an attempt to demonstrate the Bolton theory but is disappointing. Three textbooks embody the Bolton concept: J. F. Bannon, *History of the Americas* (2 vols., 1963) ; H. E. Davis, *The Americas in History* (1953) ; and V. B. Holmes, *A History of the Americas: From Discovery to Nationhood* (1950).

ENGLISH AMERICA

Two fundamental sources for any student of English colonial America are C. M. Andrews, *The Colonial Period of American History* (4 vols., 1934-1938) and L. H. Gipson, *The British Empire Before the American Revolution* (12 vols., 1936-1965).

For colonial beginnings see J. T. Adams, *The Founding of New England* (1921); C. M. Andrews, *Our Earliest Colonial Settlements* (1933); W. F. Craven, *The Southern Colonies in the Seventeenth Century* (1947); S. E. Morison, *Builders of the Bay Colony* (1930); W. Notestein, *The English People on the Eve of Colonization, 1603-1630* (1954); A. L. Rowse, *The Elizabethans and America* (1959); and T. J. Wertenbaker, *The First Americans* (1938).

No broad analytic discussion of English colonial administration has yet appeared, but O. M. Dickerson, *American Colonial Government, 1696-1765* (1912) and L. W. Labaree, *Royal Government in America* (1930) are useful. For English colonial economic policy and trade see C. M. Andrews, *The Colonial Background of the American Revolution* (1924); B. Bailyn, *New England Merchants in the Seventeenth Century* (1955); G. L. Beer, *The Old Colonial System, 1660-1754* (1912) and *Origins of the British Colonial System* (1908); O. M. Dickerson's revisionist, *The Navigation Acts and the American Revolution* (1951); and L. A. Harper, *The English Navigation Laws* (1939).

English colonial society has had many interpreters, but some of the more provocative works are D. Boorstin, *The Americans: The Colonial Experience* (1958); and Carl Bridenbaugh, *Cities in Revolt: Urban Life in America, 1743-1776* (1955) and *Cities in the Wilderness: The First Century of Urban Life in America, 1625-1742* (1938). The best analysis of English attitudes toward the Indian is Chapter I of Roy H. Pearce, *The Savages of America: A Study of the Indian and the Idea of Civilization* (1953) and Alden Vaughan, *The Puritan Frontier* (1965). On colonial labor see Abbot E. Smith's excellent, *Colonists in Bondage: White Servitude and Convict Labor in America, 1607-1776* (1947).

On colonial intellectual life the best general work besides that of L. B. Wright is Max Savelle, *Seeds of Liberty: The Genesis of the American Mind* (1948). On more specialized aspects of the cultural scene see P. Miller, *The New England Mind: From Colony to Province* (1954) and *The New England Mind: The Seventeenth Century* (1939); S. E. Morison, *The Intellectual Life of Colonial New England* (1956); and V. L. Parrington, *Main Currents in American Thought: The Colonial Mind* (1927).

French America

For French Canada the literature in English is limited, but fortunately, the historiography of works in both French and English has been the subject of an exhaustive, critical review article by John C. Rule, "The Old

Regime in America: A Review of Recent Interpretations of France in America," *William and Mary Quarterly,* 3rd series, XIX (October, 1963), 575-600.

The nineteenth-century works of Francis Parkman are significant as much for their literary merit as for their historical value: *Count Frontenac and New France under Louis XIV* (cent. ed., 1922); *Half Century of Conflict* (1892); *The Jesuits in North America* (1867); *La Salle and the Discovery of the Great River* (1898); *The Old Regime in Canada* (1874); and *Pioneers of France in the New World* (1865). Moralistic yet romantic, Parkman highlighted the French colonial endeavor in the New World for future generations.

Parkman has been followed by more scholarly observers. General works on New France are W. B. Munro, *Crusaders of New France* (1918); R. G. Thwaites, editor of the monumental *Jesuit Relations, France in America* (1905); and G. M. Wrong, *The Rise and Fall of New France* (1928). The best recent work on French Canada has been translated from the French: Gustave Lanctôt, *The History of Canada* (3 vols., 1963-1965), a fount of information written from the French-Canadian point of view.

A number of works can be recommended for specialized subjects. On the seigneurs see W. B. Munro, *Seigneurs of Old Canada* (1915) and *The Seignorial System in Canada* (1927). H. A. Innis, *The Fur Trade in Canada* (1956) is an excellent discussion of this subject, while the early economic development of French Canada is analyzed in H. P. Biggar, *The Early Trading Companies of New France* (1901). For the social history of New France see A. L. Burt, *The Old Province of Quebec* (1939); S. D. Clark, *The Social Development of Canada* (1942); C. W. Colby, *Canadian Types of the Old Regime* (1908); and the early chapters of Mason Wade, *The French Canadians 1760-1945* (1955). To balance Parkman with a more modern interpretation on the Indian in French Canada see J. H. Kennedy, *Jesuit and Savage in New France* (1950). W. J. Eccles, *Frontenac: The Courtier Governor* (1959) sets a high standard of scholarship.

SPANISH AMERICA

For the Spanish background to colonization R. B. Merriman's, *The Rise of the Spanish Empire in the Old World and the New* (4 vols., 1914-1938) is exceedingly useful from the Middle Ages to the end of the sixteenth century. Silvio Zavala's, *New Viewpoints in the Spanish Coloniza-*

tion of America (1943) presents a series of provocative essays on the theoretical framework of the conquest and colonization and fits well with J. H. Parry's, *The Spanish Theory of Empire in the Sixteenth Century* (1940).

For the Spanish conquests in America there are a number of books which will introduce the student to the conqueror and his mystique: F. A. Kirkpatrick, *The Spanish Conquistadores* (1934); W. H. Prescott's classics, *The Conquest of Mexico* and *The Conquest of Peru* (many editions); and I. B. Richman, *The Spanish Conquerors* (1919).

Spanish colonial institutions and administration are discussed in E. G. Bourne's pioneering work, *Spain in America* (1904), but Clarence Haring's *The Spanish Empire in America* (1947) superseded Bourne and remains the fundamental work on the administration and institutional aspects of the Spanish Empire. Spanish colonial economic life and trade has had a number of analysts: W. H. Borah, *Early Colonial Trade and Navigation between Mexico and Peru* (1944), *New Spain's Century of Depression* (1951), and *Silk Raising in Colonial Mexico* (1943); Earl J. Hamilton, *American Treasure and the Price Revolution in Spain, 1501-1650* (1934); Clarence Haring, *Trade and Navigation between Spain and the Indies in the Time of the Hapsburgs* (1918); L. B. Simpson, *The Encomienda System in New Spain* (1950); and Robert S. Smith, *The Spanish Guild Merchant* (1940). On the Indian, L. Hanke, *The Spanish Struggle for Justice in the Conquest of America* (1949) is fundamental for the theory behind the subjugation of the Indians, while Charles Gibson, *The Aztecs under Spanish Rule, 1519-1821* (1964) emphasizes the institutions used by the Spaniards to bring the natives under their tutelage. On the Negro, Frank Tannenbaum's, *Slave and Citizen: The Negro in the Americas* (1947) demonstrates the rewards of comparative study. The early chapters of J. L. Mecham, *Church and State in Latin America* (1934) are excellent on this subject, while H. C. Lea's, *The Inquisition in the Spanish Dependencies* (1908) is a surprisingly dispassionate assessment of this institution. Fundamental also are the demographic studies of Central Mexico by W. Borah, S. Cook, and L. B. Simpson, published in the *Ibero-Americana* series at the University of California.

Spanish colonial culture is best viewed through the works of John Tate Lanning, *Academic Culture in the Spanish Colonies* (1940) and *The University in the Kingdom of Guatemala* (1955); Irving Leonard, *Books of the Brave* (1949); and A. P. Whitaker, ed., *Latin America and the Enlightenment* (1942).